The Christian Adventure

Morris Maddocks has been Bishop of Selby since 1972. He is also Co-Chairman of the Churches' Council for Health and Healing, President of the Divine Healing Mission and Bishop Visitor to Burrswood. He is the author of *The Christian Healing Ministry*.

D1613113

Morris Maddocks
BISHOP OF SELBY

The Christian Adventure

TRI∧NGLE

F29/222

117530

First published 1983
Triangle
SPCK
Holy Trinity Church
Marylebone Road
London NW1 4DU

British Library Cataloguing in Publication Data

Maddocks, Morris
  The Christian adventure.
  1. Christian life
  I. Title
  248.4   BV4501.2
  ISBN 0-281-04032-X

Filmset, printed and bound in Great Britain by
Hazell Watson & Viney Ltd, Aylesbury, Bucks

CONTENTS

INTRODUCTION

The Spirit of Adventure

'Life is an adventure directed by God.' In those words Paul
Tournier summed up one of the chapters in his book *The
Adventure of Living*, which happened to be about the lessons of
failure. It was an encouraging book to read in the mid-sixties;
many at that time were less so. In this little book of Bible
meditations I want to look at life in terms of *Christian adventure*.

The instinct of adventure is part of man's make-up. It is
endemic to his personality. It is the motive force behind the
energy man displays in invention and discovery. Look back to the
history of our island race. What is it that has driven great men
over the seas on voyages of discovery or to defend our coasts from
enemy invaders? What has made men persevere relentlessly in
mechanical and scientific research until the day comes when all
falls into place: a new idea, a new formula, a new machine is
born? And still man is driven on. 'Strife alone pleases us and not
the victory;' wrote Pascal, 'we never seek things in themselves,
but only the search for things.'

Nowhere is this instinct given such full play as in the spiritual
dimension to life. Art and music lead mankind into adventures
beyond his consciousness; so does religion.

Of course religion can become so structured, and eventually
ossified, that all instinct for adventure is killed. But Christianity—
and it is the Christian adventure with which we are concerned—
is designed to bring men and women freedom, 'the glorious liberty
of the children of God', and we are to live in this liberty wherewith
Christ has made us free.

One most powerful illustration of a rebirth of this instinct of
adventure is to be found in the life of St Paul. As Saul of Tarsus
he had been constrained by the Law; he enjoyed no freedom in
his religion; he had to conform to the minutiae of his religion's
regulations and he saw to it that others did so too. In fact it was
on such a mission of constraint that he was confronted by the
risen Christ. This experience, usually called the conversion of St
Paul, was for him the beginning of freedom, a moment in which
his instinct for adventure was reborn. His baptism and the gift of
the Spirit completed what was for him a new Pentecost, and it
seems he was filled particularly with the spirit of adventure. From
that moment onwards he was *driven* (cf. Luke 4.1) relentlessly on

in the Christian adventure of spreading the good news of Jesus Christ. He faced every hardship, as we shall see later on, encountered every difficulty, met every sort of danger, but still he went on. His life could be called one long Christian adventure.

We learn therefore that becoming a Christian is similar to being born again, as Jesus told Nicodemus (John 3), followed by a steady growth into Christ. At each stage and deepening of experience, the spirit of adventure also receives a new freedom in us. The Holy Spirit, who is the Spirit of Movement and Adventure, is always calling us to look forward, and if we are sensitive to his pressures, we find he is always leading and driving us on. He fans into flame the spark of that instinct already within us, 'inspiring' us to attempt great things for the glory of God, equipping and empowering us for the Christian adventure.

Suggestions on how to use this book

The book can be used as a six-week Bible study. There are special readings on prayer for the first five Sundays, followed by studies for each weekday, on a weekly theme relating to the Christian adventure. For the most part the themes are illustrated from biblical personalities, whose lives were classic adventures for God.

The sixth week looks at Jesus and his very special adventure for mankind. It is set within the framework of Holy Week, so that it begins and also ends with Sundays—Palm Sunday and Easter Day.

The book can therefore also be used as a Lent book. For this purpose I have added preliminary studies for the first four days of Lent. The six weeks then follow on as the six weeks of Lent, culminating in Holy Week and Easter Day.

In these studies we shall watch how God calls his servants to the adventure of a life lived entirely for him (Week 1), how he calls them to a deep commitment and how they respond (Week 2). We shall see again the necessity of communication through prayer during the adventure and how these prayers are answered (Week 3). The love that constantly enfolds those who undertake the adventure then leads us to see that God himself is love and the inspiration of the whole of life (Week 4). The sharing and spreading of this good news, for which God's servants are equipped with the spirit of adventure, is then seen as the normal and essential purpose of life for which Christians are 'anointed' by the Spirit (Week 5).

Finally we are led to take a share in some of the epoch-making events of Jesus' earthly life—in Christ's own 'adventure' culminating in the momentous events of the Passion/Resurrection, the mighty work of the New Covenant, showing forth the divine adventure of redemption to which God had committed himself once he had created 'all things well' and man 'in his own image'.

The last two Sundays (I have included a meditation for Easter Day) are part of this last week's events. The other Sundays are different, as Sunday, the day of the resurrection and of rest, is different from other days of the week. I have provided some suggestions for quiet reading and reflection.

The main part of the book is a commentary or series of comments on the scriptural passage chosen for each weekday. It is hoped that, after reading the passage of Scripture and comment, some time will be given to reflect on the passage and/or on the suggested theme for reflection before offering the closing prayer. The whole may take 15 to 20 minutes. I have used the New International Version (NIV) of the Bible throughout. I have also added some prayers that may be used, singly or together, before and after this or any other time of prayer.

Try to be relaxed and in a comfortable position during this time, to find an oasis of stillness and quiet (sometimes not all that easy), and if possible offer the best time of the day to God—early morning for preference.

So that these meditations may also be used by a house group, Lent group, prayer or study group, I have included some questions for each week. Let each member of the group use the studies individually at home and when the group gathers week by week, each member could have been assigned 'a day', on which they will lead, giving their own comments and ideas, and then the group can take one or more of the questions to discuss in the light of individual contributions. A resolution for action could be taken by the group, which is then offered in prayer.

My own offering of prayer is that this book may be used by the Lord in furthering the great work *he* is doing among us at the present time and that it may help us to experience even more fully the joy of being part of the great adventure for Christ.

I should like to thank SPCK for the honour of the invitation to write this book, and especially Myrtle Powley, my editor, for her counsel.

As always I am grateful to Archbishop Stuart Blanch for his encouragement to take the opportunity of writing (and reading) and to my colleagues and friends in the York diocese, and further afield, for their understanding and prayer. Also to Mrs June Hall, my secretary, who has once again typed and corrected the manuscript.

As ever I am abundantly grateful to my wife Anne for her patient love and prayerful support, and since she has helped me with some of the devotional material, we should like to dedicate this book together as an act of gratitude to the members of our Healing Prayer Fellowships and to the Crowhurst Community who looked after us during our writing of the major part of the book.

+ MORRIS SELBY

Upper Poppleton, York
St Peter's Day 1982

PRAYERS BEFORE AND
AFTER MEDITATION

BEFORE MEDITATION

Speak Lord, for your servant is listening.

1 Samuel 3.10

Father, as we come to adore you,
   grant us to hear your Word so attentively
      to experience the power of the Spirit so luminously
  that we may be healed inwardly, deeply and eternally.   Amen.

Almighty God and Father, help us to be still in your presence,
that we may know ourselves to be your people,
and you to be our God;
through Jesus Christ our Lord.   Amen.

James M. Todd

O gracious and holy Father,
   Give us wisdom to perceive thee,
      intelligence to understand thee,
      diligence to seek thee,
      patience to wait for thee,
      eyes to behold thee,
      a heart to meditate upon thee,
      and a life to proclaim thee;
  through the power of the Spirit of Jesus Christ our Lord.
   Amen.

St Benedict

AFTER MEDITATION

Father, may we go forth in the Name of your Son Jesus Christ,
   ransomed, healed, restored and forgiven,
   and in the power of the Holy Spirit,
   enabled and equipped for your service,
   this day and every day.   Amen.

Be, Lord,
   within me to strengthen me
   without me to preserve me
   over me to shelter me
   beneath me to support me
   before me to divert me
   behind me to bring me back
   round about me to fortify me.   Amen.

Bishop Andrewes

Now to him who is able to do immeasurably more than all we ask
or imagine, according to his power that is at work within us, to
him be glory in the church and in Christ Jesus throughout all
generations, for ever and ever!   Amen.

Ephesians 3.20–1

PRELIMINARY STUDIES

The Testing of Vocation

The testing of Jesus
MATTHEW 4.1–11

Today we begin our journey with Jesus, our sharing of his testing, passion and death, that will culminate in 'being partakers with him of his resurrection' on Easter Day. We shall use these first four days to ponder on the testing of vocation by way of preparation for the adventure of following Jesus. Let us begin with *his* testing.

The gospel account of Jesus' temptations is a *legendum*, something needing to be read, words which will speak to us of Christ's struggle with the world's pressures. The quotations come from the literary deposit of the age-old encounter between Satan and God's chosen people. Israel had been tested in the wilderness; Jesus was driven by the Spirit on to the same testing ground. It was an unpropitious start to his ministry, but as God used the cross, so did he use the testing in the wilderness. The material for defeat was transformed into the very substance of victory. What do the three temptations of Jesus teach us about our discipleship today?

First temptation: To get along under my own steam.

Remedy: To become dependent on the word of God.

Our initial zest in Christ's service, our youth and high spirits, are a splendid springboard for life and enable us to 'thrust out a little from the land'. But we need more than our own steam to 'launch out into the deep'. The further we go in the adventure of life, especially out of our depth, the closer we need to wait upon the Lord, to listen and keep on listening to his promptings, to weigh every decision, every action by 'every word that comes from the mouth of God'. This very first test points to a remedy that we shall endeavour to take on board our life until it becomes part of it—a constant waiting on the Lord, attuned to his will, so that prayer becomes our life and our life becomes prayer. We shall seek the word at *his* mouth, not our own. The next few weeks will be a time of special listening to *his* word, enabling us to become dependent on *THE* Word.

Second temptation: To take needless risks in the adventure of life and faith.

Remedy: To trust God for everything, at every point, every day.

God is all powerful and is at hand to everyone and everything. But it is dangerous to presume upon his love and will to save us. He is not going to rescue us automatically, especially if we have not respected the life he has given us. And if he does rescue us, he will not leave us unchanged. If we touch the hem of his garment, he will do more for us than heal our broken finger. His touch will not only impress us: it will heal us. He will change us at the centre. We can therefore trust him, completely and utterly, as he trusted his heavenly Father.

Third temptation: To worship false gods (idolatry).

Remedy: To worship the only true God, single-mindedly.

There are plenty of opportunities to take short cuts to power, to gain it by the devil's means. This may be at the expense of my brother, or by means of lies and false statements and actions, or by compromise. We are not in business however to come to terms with the world's standards, but rather to present God's standards to the world. Jesus showed that there could be no compromise in the message of the Kingdom. By all the means at his disposal— by preaching, teaching and healing, and eventually by the cross, he would give his all for the life of the world to the glory of God the Father. Can we do anything less?

This requires total single-mindedness. 'Seek *first* his Kingdom' (Matt. 6.33). It will therefore involve a reordering of our priorities, in turn bringing a change in our lifestyle and attitudes. We shall in fact be tested.

It will throw us completely on the mercy of God. We shall gradually become totally dependent on *him* (1): we shall learn to trust *him* for everything (2): our worship (which includes all life) will indeed be single-minded (3).

Reflect on

Christianity is not a code of conduct. It does not mean simply being polite to aunts and kind to animals. Christianity is exposure to love—exposure to this power more searing than any radiation. It does not involve learning a list of rules. It involves laying oneself open to God who is love, recognizing that love is the beginning and the end, believing that 'this is the famous stone that turneth all to gold', accepting that love may throw one's attitudes and values upside down, and yielding to the worst that love may do. Love was his meaning. Love is his nature. And Love is his name.

Jack Burton, *Transport of Delight*, p.10

Prayer

Almighty God,
whose Son Jesus Christ fasted forty days in the wilderness,
and was tempted as we are, yet without sin:
give us grace to discipline ourselves
    in obedience to your Spirit;
and, as you know our weakness,
so may we know your power to save;
through Jesus Christ our Lord.   Amen.

Collect for Lent 1 (ASB)

The testing of Abraham
GENESIS 22.1–19

One of the finest pieces of Hebrew prose narrative in the Old Testament, this passage is a prophetic protest against the ancient custom of child sacrifice, which the Hebrews tragically learned from their neighbours during the early years of their settlement in Canaan.

Just as we shall see on Saturday how there came a time when Jesus considered Peter was ready for testing, so now God saw that Abraham had reached that point in his spiritual development. The question is, has Abraham that necessary edge of steel in his faith on which God can depend to found his chosen people? (Jesus must have asked himself the same question of Peter.) The complete surrender of Abraham's response showed he had; God was able to reaffirm the Promise, because Abraham had undergone a symbolic death in perfect obedience to God's demand. For the writer, this was the supreme moment in Abraham's spiritual pilgrimage. 'Take your son, your only son . . . sacrifice him' (v.2). As God calls out his people to follow him (the Greek word for 'church', *ecclesia*, refers to those 'called out' by God, a process that finds its origins in Abraham's call), there is always a point of reference to God's very own Son, who was called to be Jesus, the Saviour, who would die to save the world. This story has obvious and prophetic parallels. From the first there must have been an agony of foreknowledge in the heart of God.

v.7f: 'Where is the lamb for the burnt offering?' 'God himself will provide the lamb for the burnt offering.' The poignant question of the boy and the succinct, yet trustful, reply of his father underline the pathos of the story as well as its prophetic content, especially for us at the beginning of this course of study. As we begin our spiritual adventure and testing, we look forward across the weeks to the death and resurrection of Jesus, the testing of God's own Son. 'Behold the Lamb of God.' He is the Lamb provided by God, both for the sacrifice on the cross and as a symbol (with flag) of the risen Christ.

v.12: 'Now I know that you fear God.' The test was passed. Abraham had not withheld his son, his most precious possession, from God. He had undergone a thousand deaths and come through. The adventure for God had been a test fraught with risks, in fact a matter of life and death. In this prophetic story, we are given the assurance that life always follows death.

v.18: '. . . because you have obeyed me.' The second call from the angel of the Lord was a promise of blessing for Abraham, his descendants and for the nations of the earth through them. His obedience, like Mary's (tomorrow's reading), was a sure foundation for God's work of redemption.

Reflect on
'At the very outset of the salvation history, through the faith and obedience of one man, the whole pattern of redemption is prefigured.'
The leaves on the tree will be for the healing of the nations.

Prayer
Almighty God,
by whose grace alone we are accepted
  and called to your service:
strengthen us by your Holy Spirit
and make us worthy of our calling;
through Jesus Christ our Lord.   Amen.
Collect for Epiphany 2 (ASB)

The testing of Mary
LUKE 1.26–45

This scene of the Annunciation has been the subject of many great paintings. It has also been a favourite motif in churches—Gabriel saluting Mary, usually pictured in prayer, and the Holy Spirit in the form of a dove or ray of light overshadowing Mary. Is there an annunciation scene in your church, in stained glass, in a painting or in a carving? It is frequently treated so because of the great importance of the event.

Here is the first decisive act of God's redemption. God sends his Son to be the world's Saviour: v.31, 'You are to give him the name Jesus' (i.e. Saviour). He will be great, called the Son of the Most High, of David's descent, ruler of Israel and be given an eternal Kingdom. Little wonder Mary was troubled.

The whole passage of course in fact centres on Mary; *let us ponder on this divine adventure placed before her, on her guarded and questioning response, on her reassurance and on her final response of utter commitment.*

1   The angel greets Mary in a way that shows her to be the recipient of a special grace of God. (This salutation has become a favourite prayer of Christians down the ages.) The angel messenger also connects the event in the mind of the reader with the previous narrative—the announcement of the forthcoming birth of John, Jesus' forerunner (vv.26–8).

2   In answer to Mary's troubled countenance, the angel gives her reassurance. She will have a child and that child will be extremely special, in fact the world's redeemer (vv.29–33).

3   This naturally leads to more questioning, and the facts are spelt out. The agent of conception will be God himself through his Holy Spirit. The babe will therefore be 'God, of the Substance of the Father, begotten before the worlds: and Man, of the Substance of his Mother, born in the world' (Creed of St Athanasius). The sign of the truth of this assertion was Elizabeth's conception in her old age (vv.35–7). The word for 'overshadow' is used again at the Transfiguration (Luke 9.34) and always refers to divine power.

4   The proclamation of this glorious mystery, the virginal conception, elicits the perfect response from Mary, one of self-giving obedience for which God had been waiting from the

beginning, a reversal of Eve's disobedience. 'I am the Lord's servant. May it be to me as you have said' (v.38).

The test has been undergone and Mary is within the divine will. Her state of grace is affirmed by her cousin Elizabeth: 'Blessed is she who has believed that what the Lord has said to her will be accomplished' (v.45). The Christian adventure so often begins with an acceptance of the way God sets before us, and an acceptance in our heart that that is *the right way, because it is his way*.

Reflect on

This is that blessed Mary, pre-elect
   God's Virgin. Gone is a great while, and she
   Dwelt young in Nazareth of Galilee.
Unto God's will she brought devout respect,
Profound simplicity of intellect,
   And supreme patience. From her mother's knee,
   Faithful and hopeful; wise in charity;
Strong in grave peace; in pity circumspect.

So held she through her girlhood; as it were
   An angel-watered lily, that near God
   Grows, and is quiet. Till, one dawn at home
She woke in her white bed, and had no fear
   At all,—yet wept till sunshine, and felt awed:
   Because the fulness of the time was come.
Dante Gabriel Rossetti

Act of Praise

The Magnificat (Luke 1.46–55)

The testing of Peter
MATTHEW 16.13–28

Peter's testing opens up the way for Jesus to deepen the disciples' understanding of the adventure entailed in following him. From this experience they learn that the Christ will model his ministry on the suffering servant (see Isaiah 52.13—53.12) and that the way he intends to travel will lead to a cross.

The place of testing, as in the case of Jesus' own temptations (see Wednesday), was once again 'the wilderness', for they were on the unreceptive soil of pagan territory. Caesarea Philippi, formerly Paneas after the god Pan, was rebuilt by the tetrarch Philip and renamed after Caesar, and himself. It continued to be a pagan city and Jesus did not enter it, but stayed 'in the district'.

Jesus used this time of withdrawal for questioning his disciples closely and for giving them important teaching. The episode marks a turning point in the gospels. (Cf. Mark 8.27ff.; Luke 9.18ff.)

1 'Who do you say I am?' (v.15). After the close questioning concerning what others think, Jesus points the finger directly at the disciples—'But *you* . . .' At some stage in our discipleship, that very direct question is directed to each one of us. What about *you*? Can we from our heart match Peter's answer? He acknowledged him to be the Christ, the long-awaited, anointed Son of the living God.

2 'You are Peter (Cephas) and on this rock (*cephas*) I will build my church' (v.18). There is no assertion that it is Peter's statement of faith or any of Peter's successors that will be the foundation stone. Just Peter himself, the first to believe in Jesus as the Christ. That he assumed basic leadership is obvious from the early chapters of Acts as well as, for instance, from the later chapters of St John's gospel. Jesus' choice of him is as mysterious and real as God's choice of Israel. In both cases they remain the chosen instrument, despite failures and disobedience. God is able to absorb all human failings into his perfect will.

3 'That he must suffer' (v.21). This is now the recurring theme in the remainder of Jesus' ministry. His face is set like a flint (see Isaiah 50.6–7; Luke 9.51). When Peter tries to dissuade him from such a (humanly speaking) unthinkable course, he is rounded on with a stunning rebuke. The suffering is the

divine will. Anyone who diverts Jesus from the course, even his best friend, is an agent of the adversary, Satan. The constant temptation in our discipleship is to mind the things of men rather than the things of God. Have I failed in this during this week?

4 'If anyone would come after me, he must deny himself and take up his cross and follow me' (v.24). This is inevitably coloured by subsequent history. Jesus would take up his cross; his followers must be prepared to do the same. One always has the feeling that such sections on discipleship are particularly apposite for a martyr church. Peter began his adventure for Christ by showing his willingness to risk and lose his physical life.

Reflect on
'Simon, Simon, Satan has asked to sift you as wheat. But I have prayed for you, Simon, that your faith may not fail. And when you have turned back, strengthen your brothers.'
Luke 22.31f.

Prayer
Almighty God,
who inspired your apostle Saint Peter
to confess Jesus as Christ and Son of the living God:
build up your Church upon this rock,
that in unity and peace
it may proclaim one truth and follow one Lord,
your Son our Saviour Jesus Christ,
who is alive and reigns with you and the Holy Spirit,
one God, now and for ever.   Amen.
Collect for St Peter's Day (ASB)

GROUP QUESTIONS

The testing of vocation

1 What do the three temptations of Jesus teach us about our discipleship today? (Wednesday)

2 Should complete obedience be the hallmark of contemporary discipleship? (Thursday and Friday) How do we discern God's will today?

3 'Who do you say I am?' What would we answer if Jesus faced us with this question? Would our life and witness support our words? (Saturday)

4 Was there any other way than the cross for Jesus? Is there any other way for us to follow him? (Saturday)

WEEK ONE

Read   1 Thessalonians 5.16–24

Reflect on
To live in prayer, therefore, is to live in the Spirit, and to live in the Spirit is to live in Christ. I am not saying that prayer is a means or a method which we have to use in order to have more of Christ in us or in order to be more fully possessed by the Spirit. I am saying something simpler and more fundamental: to live in Christ is to live in prayer. Prayer is not something you do; it is a style of living. It is living under the witness which the Spirit bears with our spirit that we are sons of God. Such a witness lays upon us the awful freedom of adult sonship. Prayer is our response to both the privilege and the responsibility whereby we cry Abba, Father! To engage in the mission of God, therefore, is to live this life of prayer; praying without ceasing, as St Paul puts it, that is to say, sustaining a style of life that is focused upon God. This is indeed to engage in the mission of the Holy Spirit by being rather than by doing. To realize that the heart of mission is communion with God in the midst of the world's life will save us from the demented activism of these days.
John V. Taylor, *The Go-Between God*, p.226f.

Prayer
Father, I pray that today I may know with keener awareness that I am in your hands. Well or ill, happy or sad, at work or at leisure, with others or alone, may I become increasingly conscious that you, who have called me, are utterly trustworthy and will accomplish your purpose in me. Grant me the sense of your presence, born of your indwelling and enfolding love.

If this week brings storm or stress, fear or sorrow, pain or disappointment, or if it brings gladness, serenity, happiness and peace, let nothing rob me of the joy of knowing I am yours, kept by your power in readiness for the coming of our Lord Jesus Christ.   Amen.
After a prayer by Leslie Weatherhead

The Call to Adventure

The call of Abraham
GENESIS 12.1–9

The Bible has been called a record of the God who calls. To many he speaks directly and insistently. We shall notice the suddenness, almost abruptness of God's call this week; also the expectancy that the response will be unhesitating and immediate.

There is always an urgency about his call and it is always for a purpose—to fulfil God's purpose. It therefore takes the person out of his natural environment, singles him out, while gradually he is equipped to fulfil that purpose. A further point is that the initiative is always with God. 'You did not choose me, but I chose you' (John 15.16) is true for all who hear God's call.

Abraham is the first real personality we meet in the Bible. Although he is in some sense a type of the man of faith, yet a case can be made for his historicity, while the narrative art of the writer makes him live as a person.

1 *The call* to serve God always demands sacrifice and for many that will entail leaving home and all that is held dear and familiar (v.1; cf. Matt. 10.37–9). It is a call impossible to disobey and must be answered at once. God's time is now. Tomorrow will be too late. What about my answer?

2 *The purpose of the call* (vv.2,3). The writer, conscious of Israel's great calling to be the light to the Gentile nations, sees the beginning of that missionary purpose in the call of the nation's first and foremost ancestor: 'All peoples on earth will be blessed through you'. How much of the adventure of mission is there in my own calling?

3 *The pilgrimage of life* (vv.4–9). Apparently Abraham traversed the land from north to south, the land of promise into which Joshua would later lead the people of Israel, without settling anywhere and without making contact with the ethnic movements of the land. A stop was made at 'the site of the great tree of Moreh at Shechem'. It was the terebinth, an evergreen, and literally translated the passage reads 'the terebinth of the teacher', a tree at which divine teaching was given, rather like the Saxon preaching crosses of the Christian

era. Here God appeared to the patriarch who 'built an altar to the Lord'.

If our 'adventure' is to have direction and purpose there must be necessary pauses in each of our lives to 'stop, look and listen' as to what the word of God has to say to us. Abraham became a man of faith because he constantly listened to and heard the word of God. This listening is an ongoing commitment for those who once answer the call. Have I neglected to answer any 'promptings' from the Lord in the past week? A continuing, listening awareness of his call is part of the Christian adventure.

Reflect on

'By faith Abraham, when called to go to a place he would later receive as his inheritance, obeyed and went, even though he did not know where he was going'
Hebrews 11.8

Prayer

Almighty God,
whose chosen servant Abraham
faithfully obeyed your call
and rejoiced in your promise
that, in him, all the families of the earth should be blessed:
give us a faith like his,
that, in us, your promises may be fulfilled;
through Jesus Christ our Lord.   Amen.
Collect for 7th Sunday before Christmas (ASB)

The call of Moses
EXODUS 3.1–20

There is an unexplained silence between the end of Genesis and the beginning of Exodus. A period of over two hundred years elapsed between the death of Joseph and the birth of Moses. What happened to the strong faith in the God of Abraham, Isaac and Jacob through those silent years?

In the present story we see that the faith had not died out entirely. For here at the burning bush it is that same God who appears to Moses, calling him to one of the greatest adventures of all history, the leading of God's people from the slavery of Egypt, through the Red Sea waters, through the wilderness on what must have seemed an interminable journey, to the very borders of the promised land.

1 *The call.* God called to him from within the bush, 'Moses, Moses'. And Moses said, 'Here I am'. Moses answers at once, as in all the biblical responses to God's call. Fire is a common form of divine manifestation, e.g. the fire on the heads of the apostles in Acts 2. Moses too needed an 'anointing' by fire for his great task. In him the history of Israel began: he was the originator both of her national life and her religion.

2 *The God who calls.* 'I am the God of your father, the God of Abraham ... Isaac... and Jacob.' 'I will be with you.' 'I am who I am' or 'I will be what I will be' (vv.6, 12 and 14; cf Rev. 1.8). His indeed are all times. He is the God who 'was', the God of our fathers, the God of the Patriarchs. He is from everlasting. He is the God who 'is', reigning in the present, the God who is always 'with us', Emmanuel, 'a very *present* help in trouble'. He is the God who 'will be', the God of the future, who has all history in his hands, even *my* future.
So the Christ who calls us today is the Christ who *has* died, the Christ who *is* risen and the Christ who *will* come again.

3 *The reason and purpose of the call.* 'I have indeed seen the misery of my people in Egypt.' 'I am sending you to Pharaoh to bring my people the Israelites out of Egypt' (vv.7 and 10). The concern for justice and the hatred of oppression are the reasons for this divine intervention, this unfolding of a new era in God's dealings with Israel and so with mankind. It is one of the great themes of the Old Testament revelation of God, reaching its climax in the eighth-century prophets'

concern for justice (Amos and Micah) and holiness (Isaiah I) and love (Hosea). The reason for the Exodus prefigured that for the cross and resurrection—the bringing of God's people out of darkness into his own marvellous light, from the slavery of sin into the glorious liberty of the children of God, from the death into life.

Reflect on
The burning bush was a life-changing, world-changing sign penetrating the secularity of a people in bondage and breaking open the mind of a man long since trapped in the routines of daily existence and, worse still, contented with them. Something new and unpredictable but highly significant happened, and we who live out our lives three thousand years and more after that event are different people because of it.

Stuart Blanch, *The Burning Bush*, p.109

Prayer
Lord God our redeemer,
who heard the cry of your people
and sent your servant Moses to lead them out of slavery:
free us from the tyranny of sin and death
and, by the leading of your Spirit,
bring us to our promised land;
through Jesus Christ our Lord.   Amen.

Collect for 6th Sunday before Christmas (ASB)

The call of Samuel
1 SAMUEL 3.1–21

We can gauge the importance of Samuel by looking at the first and last verses of this chapter. At the beginning we are told that 'in those days the word of the Lord was rare; there were not many visions'. Samuel however received a vision which is vividly and fully described by the writer. Accordingly at the end of the chapter we read: 'The Lord was with Samuel as he grew up, and he let none of his words fall to the ground' ('made everything that Samuel said come true'—TEV). Also we learn that Samuel 'was attested as a prophet of the Lord' and 'the Lord continued to appear at Shiloh' and 'revealed himself to Samuel through his word'.

As Dr Stuart Blanch points out, 'there is a sense in which Samuel stands as the fountain head of both law and prophecy; . . . it is also true that he was accepted and honoured as a judge.' Like the great eighth-century prophets after him, he interpreted the events of the day, the personal and the political, in the light of the Torah (law of God). 'Not a new idea of God, but a new encounter with God, is the essence and basis of prophetic preaching' (Kittel). Samuel's own encounter with God enabled him to lead the people into a new experience of the God of their fathers. He inaugurated a new era in the spiritual adventure and pilgrimage of Israel.

1 *The setting*. The writer vividly sets the scene. The sadness of Eli's old age, the youth of his servant Samuel. 'The lamp of God had not yet gone out' (v.3) is a highly symbolic turn of phrase. Samuel lies down 'where the ark of God was': but he is the one who will now stay close to the law and word of God, the last of the judges and the first of the prophets.

2 *The three-fold call*. The Lord called: Samuel went straight to his (earthly) master. 'Here I am; you called me' (vv.5,6,8). He 'did not yet know the Lord' (v.7). Only after the three calls did Eli instruct him what to say. The name Samuel sounds like the Hebrew for 'heard of God'.

3 *The prayer of listening, of attentive regard*. 'Speak, Lord, for your servant is listening' (vv.9 and 10). This classic prayer has caused men and women to be open to the Lord's will down the ages. It was prayed by St Paul after his great vision on the Damascus road (Acts 22.10) and has been echoed by many of

God's people before and since. It leads to a discernment of where and how our life can be enfolded within the will of God. It could be a helpful preliminary to all our praying, meditation and contemplation. If we have not done so already, could we make it part of our daily life?

Reflect on

Coming to terms with silence is a necessary element in self-knowledge and in prayer. Pascal claimed that 'most of man's troubles come from his not being able to sit quietly in his room'.

The purpose of silence is to allow the heart to be still and to listen to God. To build up inner resources of silence and stillness is one of the central tasks of training in prayer. In a culture which has almost outlawed silence, it is a matter of urgency that Christians create oases, centres in which inner silence can be cultivated.

from Kenneth Leech, *Soul Friend*

Prayer

As you continued to appear at Shiloh,
So withdraw not your mercy from our home and community
But be our constant guest:
As you revealed yourself to Samuel through your word,
So continue to assure us of your presence
And through our reading and hearing of your word,
Our silence and our stillness,
Guide us and give us discernment in all things.
Speak, Lord, your servant is listening—today.

The call of Isaiah
ISAIAH 6.1–13

Here we have Isaiah's own personal record of his call, as dramatic as St Paul's recounted in Acts 22 and 26. It set before Isaiah the ideal of prophecy as a life-work; his ministry was to be total, something that required complete personal commitment in the Lord's service. His whole life was to be an adventure for God. It was also to be unsuccessful. The people would be 'ever hearing, but never understanding; ever seeing, but never perceiving'. If it were otherwise, they would 'turn and be healed' (vv.9 and 10).

This must have been something of a shock to the youthful enthusiasm of Isaiah. A young man of some intellect, who cared deeply for his people and more so for his God, would undoubtedly perceive the need of contemporary society for healing. It had grown corrupt and gone away from its religion of the heart. The young Isaiah caught a vision of the holiness of his God who demanded a like holiness in his people. Surely they would see this. But no; they have dull ears and closed eyes (cf. v.10 note in NIV). There's none so deaf as those who don't want to hear, or blind as those who refuse to see!

But for now, the vision and the call are everything. And Isaiah was given grace to cling on to them through his life, even in moments of depression and despair. This passage could frequently be a great encouragement in our own lives, especially when our enthusiasm for the Christian adventure wears thin. It was to me on the day of my ordination, and has been ever since.

1 As he worships and prays in the temple, Isaiah is given an overwhelming impression of *the immensity of God's greatness*. High and exalted, God was adored by the seraph choirs who chanted to each other about the holiness of God and how he reveals his glory in the world. The vision was evoked by the worship. We still sing the same song—the Tri-sanctus—today. Can it lift us heavenwards as it lifted Isaiah? (vv.1–4).

2 The vision of God always confronts us with *our own unworthiness*. 'Woe is me', cries Isaiah, conscious of his own sin and the sin of society (v.5). The holiness of God demands a like holiness both in the individual and in society.

3 Isaiah's act of contrition is followed by a symbolic cleansing to assure him of the divine pardon. *Forgiveness* alone can prepare us for service (vv.6 and 7).

4   *The call and the response.* His cleansing following the vision had prepared him to hear the call. His response links him across the centuries with God's servants: 'Here am I,' with Abraham and Samuel; '*Send* me,' with the apostles.

Reflect on

The saints, the holy ones of God, are those who through Christ's work and God's calling participate in the divine holiness; they are the individual members of the holy people of God. Like Christ they are made holy, set apart from the world. They can show forth the divine holiness or they can obscure it: they cannot either create or destroy it.

from Alan Richardson, *An Introduction to the Theology of the New Testament*

Prayer

Holy, Holy, Holy Lord,
God of power and might,
heaven and earth are full of your glory.
Hosanna in the highest.

From the Eucharistic Prayer (ASB)

The call of the disciples
LUKE 5.1–11

Luke's account of the call of the first disciples is parallel to the call of the first four in Mark 1.16–20. Mark tells the story with a characteristic economy of words. Luke here spins the story out, linking it with Jesus' teaching ministry and the story of a miraculous catch of fish (cf. John 21.1–14). For what reason?

Obviously Luke wants to give prominence to the call of Simon Peter. He therefore tells us that Jesus chooses Simon's boat (v.3) from which to speak to people. It is interesting that a boat has become one of the symbols of the Church, the deposit of sacred teaching. Jesus first used a boat as a pulpit.

But that is not all. Jesus also made Simon undertake an adventure in the deep, as if he were testing his obedience and courage. When his obedience (hasn't this been a feature of all the responses to God's call we have read this week?) resulted in a miraculous catch of fish, Simon was overwhelmed with an overpowering experience of the holiness of Jesus. As with Isaiah (yesterday), it was the holiness of the Lord that gripped the prospective disciple and gave him an inner compulsion to follow obediently in the Lord's service. Simon Peter would have the new task of 'catching men' (v.10). The story also provides a symbol of the eternal call to discipleship.

1   *'Put out a little from shore'* (v.3). From the vantage point of the boat, Jesus could see each individual in the crowd on the shore and each one could see him. It is often necessary, both at the beginning of our adventure for Christ and frequently during our life of discipleship, to take a different stance, a new vantage point, from which we may see the old familiar landmarks in a new light. In these times of 'retreat' we get things in the right perspective, dream dreams and see visions, so that the spiritual element in our personality is put to work afresh and so enlarged.

2   *'Put out into deep water'* (v.4). The command Jesus gave to Simon was calculated to test his obedience and so lead him to a new stage of spiritual maturity. The challenge to a further experience of adventure received a positive reaction and so they went out into the deep. It is only when we are out of our depth that we learn the lesson of total reliance on the grace of God. 'Lord, I'm out of my depth' is a prayer that marks a spiritual advance. And again, the only place to engage in a

profitable fishing industry is where the fish are—out in the deep. We shall not be much use as fishers of men if we insist on staying in the shallows.

3   *'Let down the nets for a catch'* (v.4). Once the right position is attained, the rest follows. How similar the life of prayer: during the journey into the deep and once there, one has to remain very close to Jesus: but everything then falls into place. Mission ('from now on you will catch men'—v.10) and discipleship ('they left everything and followed him'—v.11) become part of life.

Reflect on

And Him evermore we behold
Walking in Galilee,
Through the waving cornfields' gold,
By hamlet and wood and wold,
By the side of the marvellous sea.
He touches the sightless eyes,
Before Him the demons flee.
To the dead He sayeth, 'Arise',
To the living, 'Follow Me'.
And His voice still soundeth on
From centuries that have gone
To the centuries that shall be.
Henry Wadsworth Longfellow

Prayer

Out of the depths I cry to you, O Lord: O Lord, hear my voice.
My soul waits for the Lord, more than the watchmen wait for the morning, more than watchmen wait for the morning.
Put your hope in the Lord, for with the Lord is unfailing love
And with him is full redemption.
Psalm 130.1,6,7

The call of Saul of Tarsus
ACTS 22.3–21

The conversion of St Paul, as Saul later became, is one of the most significant events in the history of Christianity. I have chosen Paul's own account of the event, the second of the three times Luke records it in Acts, thereby underlining its supreme importance (cf. 9.1–19 and 26.9–20).

Many of Paul's previous experiences had prepared him for this mammoth turn-around (the meaning of conversion). Some of them are mentioned in this chapter: he had been a pupil of a great scholar, Gamaliel, and had previously been brought up as a pious Jew by his parents (v.3); he had persecuted many Christians and must have been impressed by their steadfastness and courage under trial (v.4); he had been an instigator and witness of the death of Stephen, and the way he died, so similar to that of his Master, cannot fail to have left an indelible mark on Paul's consciousness (v.20). His fanatical zeal in persecuting the Christians was a sure sign that Christ was winning the internal battle for his soul. It was indeed hard, and always will be, to kick against the goads.

Saul, as he then was, asked the Lord who appeared to him two questions—questions which are still basic to all our lives.

1 *'Who are you, Lord?'* (v.8). Sooner or later every one of us has to answer this question. The name Jesus means Saviour or Healer. Is he my Saviour? Have I asked him to take possession of my life? Have I allowed him to heal all my hurts, resentments, my fears, my hatreds, my bitterness? Have I allowed him to forgive all my sins? Saul had quite a few prejudices and many blind spots which Jesus had to heal before he could become the great apostle, St Paul. All this healing was a prelude to the greatest apostolic adventure of all time. Is Jesus *my* Lord? (Cf. Exod. 15.26: 'I am the Lord who heals you.')

2 *'What shall I do, Lord?'* (v.10). Once the inner change has been permitted to take place (the initiative lies with us to invite Jesus into our lives) then it will be more easy to hear what 'the still small voice' is saying. Perhaps we shall feel that we are being prompted to take a certain course of action, or to speak to someone, or to read a particular Bible passage. God has many ways of disclosing our special adventure for

him: the essential factor is that we shall be ready to hear and obey.

Metropolitan Anthony once told the story of how, as a young medical student, a colleague took him to a lecture by a priest on the Christian faith. He was annoyed by what the priest said and, on his return home, borrowed his mother's New Testament and began reading St Mark's Gospel in order to prove him wrong. He had not read many chapters before he was aware of a 'presence' on the other side of his desk. 'That presence,' he said, 'I knew to be the risen Christ, who has never left me.'

The presence of Christ risen never left St Paul. From that moment at Damascus, he was ready for his commission and tirelessly answered the call to his dying day. He willingly bore suffering for the sake of making known the glorious riches of the risen Christ, the hope of a glory to come. (See Col. 1.24–9.) Let us pray that a like energy will work in us.

Reflect on
'Who are you, Lord?'
'What shall I do, Lord?'

Prayer
Lord, you did call Saul, the persecutor of the Church,
    to be the Apostle Paul,
    to proclaim the Gospel of your Son Jesus Christ to the Gentiles:
Grant that as you have also called us,
    we may be true to our calling,
    counting everything loss for the gain of knowing Christ Jesus as our Saviour;
    for the glory of your Name.   Amen.
Church of South India liturgy (adapted)

GROUP QUESTIONS

The call to adventure

1 'How much of the adventure of mission is there in my own calling?' Do I still expect to hear and receive God's call? (Monday)

2 Why does Archbishop Blanch call the burning bush 'a life-changing, world-changing sign'? (Tuesday)

3 What are the favourable conditions required for good listening? What hinders my own attempt at listening to what God has to say to me? (Wednesday)

4 Has the holiness of God a message for today's world? How does Isaiah's response to his call help us in ours? (Thursday)

5 Did you see your call to discipleship as a call to mission? 'From now on you will catch men.' (Friday)

6 Have we seriously asked and sought answers for the questions Paul asked? 'Who are you, Lord?' 'What shall I do, Lord?' (Saturday)

WEEK TWO

Read   Philippians 4.4–8

Reflect on
The time I give to active work must be in proportion to what I give to the work of God, that is to prayer. I need more fervent and continual prayer to give character to my life. So I must give more time to meditation, and stay longer in the Lord's company, sometimes reading or saying my prayers aloud or just keeping silent. The company of Jesus will be my light, my comfort and my joy.
Pope John XXIII, *Journal of a Soul*, p.208

Prayer
Living Lord, conqueror of death, we remember with gladness how on the day of your resurrection you appeared to your disciples in your risen power and said to them, 'Peace be with you'.
Speak that word to our hearts today, O Lord.
Lift us above all our doubts and fears; and help us so to practise your presence and to rest upon your victory that your peace may be with us, now and for evermore.   Amen.
Contemporary Parish Prayers, no.131

The Adventure of Commitment

Abraham's commitment and Jahweh's Covenant
GENESIS 15

The vision (v.1) apparently refers to the whole of this chapter. Certainly Abraham appears to have experienced during this period many states of consciousness including sleep-like trance (vv.12ff.) and a state in which he enjoyed extra-sensory perception (ESP) (vv.5, 10f, 17). He also underwent several stages in his spiritual development:

1 *Assurance*. The 'after this' in v.1 refers to his renunciation of spoils of war which were rightfully his. This willingness to sacrifice his rights for a greater good is met by a promise of assurance from the Lord (v.1b).

2 *Doubt*. The problem of an heir loomed large and was a burden to Abraham. He therefore expressed his anxiety quite openly (v.2).

3 *Complaint*. He had been open about his worries. Now he openly complains to his God (v.3). We have lost the art of the prayer of complaint which the Psalmist knew so well. How much better than grumbling ceaselessly would it be if we complained directly to the Lord. At least we should be engaged in prayer!

4 *Reassurance*. The Lord answers the prayer of complaint first by reassuring him that his heir will come from his own body (v.4) and then by showing him the eastern night sky with its countless stars and galaxies. 'So shall your offspring be,' he reassures him.

5 *Commitment in faith*. The first peak of advanced spiritual development is now reached. Abraham took the Lord at his word. He trusted and totally accepted the Lord's word in a commitment of faith. As a result the Lord credited him with a likeness to the divine character: he accounted him as righteous. This is a high point not only in Abraham's spiritual development but in the spiritual pilgrimage of the human race. The relationship between God and man is beginning to be healed and the divine image in man to be restored (v.6).

6 *'The dark night of the soul.'* After a peak is reached in the spiritual life, a low point usually follows if we allow the Lord to lead us on. 'A thick and dreadful darkness' (v.12) came over Abraham and he was granted a foreknowledge of what would befall his descendants. But the darkness is that of a tunnel and the light at the far end leads us on, even when we are 'far from home', giving us hope even in the darkest place.

7 *At one with God.* The growth of the soul continues until there is a state of union with God. So the Lord makes a covenant with Abraham and his seed, a covenant finally fulfilled in the New Covenant, which *the* seed of Abraham, Christ, seals in his death and so opens the Kingdom to all believers, making it possible for all to enjoy this stage of union, God with man and man with God.

Reflect on Romans 4.13–25.

Prayer
O God, who through the passion of your Son made a new covenant of grace with mankind: grant that we who by baptism and faith have entered into that covenant may continue in faith, rejoice in hope and abound in love, as servants of our Lord and Saviour Jesus Christ. Amen.
Contemporary Parish Prayers, no. 602

The faith of Jacob
GENESIS 28.10–22

One of the best known and loved stories of the Old Testament, Jacob's ladder, appeals to our religious sense. It was the subject of a famous negro spiritual. It was the story on which Nathanael was meditating when Philip called him to come and see Jesus, who had in fact 'seen' Nathanael in the course of his meditation (John 1.47–51). The event took place at Bethel, which means 'house of God', and Jacob himself was overcome by a feeling of the numinous (vv.16 and 17). The writer uses the setting of an old Canaanite shrine to describe Jacob's first encounter with God, which is then validated as a proper place of worship by that encounter.

Of course it is all very 'incarnational' religion too. The purpose of the ladder is to suggest a symbol for the link between heaven and earth, between God and man. And the angels (that is, God's messengers) convey the idea of God coming down to dwell with man. The stone also symbolizes the dwelling place of God among men, his tabernacling among us. All of this was fulfilled in the Incarnation when 'the Word became flesh and lived for a while (tabernacled) among us' (John 1.14; cf. Phil. 2.5–11).

1 *The dream.* In primitive religions, men would go to a shrine for a night in order to dream. The dream would then be interpreted by a prophet at the shrine the next morning. Dreams, as Carl Jung has shown, are immensely important, and are therefore important in the spiritual adventure. Some say we should keep a record of our dreams. Jacob was profoundly influenced by his dream which formed a milestone on his spiritual pilgrimage. The God of his fathers took the initiative to maintain the relationship with Abraham's line and promised Jacob an inheritance as 'the dust of the earth' and that his offspring would prove a blessing to mankind (v.14). Jacob was also promised God's full protection. Such a promise evoked an attitude of complete trust in the young Jacob's heart (vv.10–15).

2 *The presence.* He was actually aware of the Lord's presence and felt a deep sense of awe. It is humbling to have even a glimpse of heaven, in the shape of an experience of the Lord's healing power or of a split-second knowledge of his presence. Life can never be quite the same again. This experience of Jacob during this vision of the night in 'the house of God' left

an indelible impression on him. He had been at 'the gate of heaven' (vv.16 and 17).

3 *The anointing.* Jacob wanted to mark the experience in perpetuity. Taking the stone he had used for his pillow he made the ancient religious act of anointing with oil. The act of anointing was used, later in the Old Testament, for the commissioning of priests and kings. Jacob used it to seal a covenant between himself and his God (vv.20–2). Eventually the Anointed One of God (i.e. the Christ) will effect the New Covenant between God and man. Jacob's adventure at Bethel prefigures the work of Christ, the Lord's Anointed, in the cross/resurrection. It was indeed 'the gate of heaven' (vv.18–22), which could only finally be unlocked by the redeeming work of Christ, who opened it 'once' and 'for all'.

Reflect on

When thou hadst overcome the sharpness of death:
Thou didst open the Kingdom of Heaven to all believers.
Thou sittest at the right hand of God:
In the glory of the Father.
Te Deum laudamus (BCP)

Prayer

O God of Jacob, by Whose hand
   Thy people still are fed;
Who through this weary pilgrimage
   Hast all our fathers led:

Our vows, our prayers, we now present
   Before Thy Throne of grace;
God of our fathers, be the God
   Of their succeeding race.

Through each perplexing path of life
   Our wandering footsteps guide;
Give us each day our daily bread,
   And raiment fit provide.

O spread Thy covering wings around,
   Till all our wanderings cease,
And at our Father's loved abode
   Our souls arrive in peace.   Amen.
P. Doddridge

Wednesday 2

The faith of the exiles
JEREMIAH 29.1–14

This pastoral letter to the exiles (written therefore shortly after 598 BC, the year of the Jewish deportation to Babylon) shows amazing vision, a deep spirit of prayerful caring and sound common sense. In fact it is unique in the Old Testament and is the precursor of the pastoral letters in the New Testament.

Jeremiah shows the Jews in exile that the whole world is God's world and that therefore they can worship God in a foreign land (contrary to the teaching of Deuteronomy). Prayer is perfectly possible (v.7) even though they are hundreds of miles from Jerusalem and its temple. Furthermore they must pray for the country of their exile and seek its peace and prosperity. And they must exercise common sense by building houses, planting gardens, marrying and having children and so increasing in number (vv.5 and 6).

The prophet then gives them a message of encouragement. Even though this agony of exile may last seventy years, God will eventually redeem his people and bring them hope. God has 'plans to prosper you and not to harm you, plans to give you hope and a future' (vv.10 and 11). Jeremiah shows himself to be a pastor of deep sensitivity and, like Barnabas in Acts, 'a son of encouragement'.

The deepest insight of Jeremiah, however, concerns the effect that such trials and tribulations will have on the exiles. His own experiences have taught him that the more one is deprived of one's own familiar surroundings the more overpowering is the underlying feeling of sadness and hopelessness, and the more intractable present problems and circumstances seem to be. So much the more then is one driven to regard one's own resources as totally insufficient and to stay entirely upon one's God. When the Psalmist came to this point of departure he asked, 'Now Lord, what do I look for?' He knew full well the only reply *at that point* was, 'My hope is in you' (Psalm 39.7).

So we find in this prophetic section of Jeremiah's letter:

> Then you will call upon me and come and pray to me,
>   and I will listen to you,
> You will seek me and find me
>   when you seek me with all your heart. (vv.12 and 13)

There is a tide in the affairs of men, which, having found them totally out of their depth, storm-tossed and helpless, carries them safely to the haven where they would be, giving them the certain experience that 'underneath are the everlasting arms'. Total adversity drives you into the arms of God. There is no other alternative then available, no other way left to travel. ' "I will be found by you", declares the Lord, "and will bring you back from captivity" ' (v.14).

How frequently our own little adversities are used in this way by the Lord to draw us to himself with bands of love. How greatly is our faith deepened and strengthened at such times, equipping us for the next stage in life's adventure. That must have been the experience of the exiles. The bread of adversity is spiritually nutritious.

Reflect on

The theme of spiritual growth is one of withdrawal followed by return. But the person who returns after the harrowing withdrawal that follows great suffering is changed, and in turn brings that change to the world around him, so that it attains to a greater measure of reality. The experience of suffering effects the inner transformation that withdrawal demands. It is a withdrawal from everything that was held to be necessary for happiness, indeed for life itself. This includes material security, supporting relationships with other people, bodily health, and intellectual certainty. In any one instance some of these are likely to be threatened more than others, but each has to be challenged in a most radical fashion before it can be transfigured.

It is a basic spiritual insight that all we possess on a purely personal level has to be taken away from us before we can know that deeper inner authority that lives in a world beyond the changes of our mortal life. This is the first great lesson of pain. But this insight must be balanced by a positive acceptance of our possessions; they are not mere illusions but gifts that God has bestowed on us. Where we err is in clinging to them as a means of personal support and identification. Only when we have been obliged to part with them on this purely acquisitive basis can they in due course be returned to us, not as things to be grasped, but as treasures from God that are transformed by our love into objects of eternal beauty. As we change, so all that appertains to us changes also, and is brought back to God, transfigured and resurrected.

Martin Israel, *The Pain that Heals*, pp.23f

Prayer

Father, mercifully look upon our infirmities;

and for the glory of your Name turn from us all those evils which we have justly deserved;

Grant that in all our troubles we may put our whole trust and confidence in your mercy,

and, perceiving your hope, evermore serve you in pureness and holiness of living,

to your honour and glory, through Jesus Christ our Lord. Amen.

The commitment of the disciples
JOHN 1.35–51

The call of five disciples, Simon, Andrew, James, John and Levi, is described in Mark 1.16–20 and 2.14. Here, in the first chapter of John's Gospel, the writer describes that of Andrew, his companion (? the beloved disciple of 13.23), Simon Peter, Philip and Nathanael.

The first two, who were obviously influenced greatly by the testimony of John the Baptist, 'Look, the Lamb of God' (v.36, and see vv.29ff.), offered to follow Jesus and were accepted. It was more of a commitment than a call. Some commentators discern a deeper meaning in the commitment, symbolic of man's quest for Christ and its outcome:

1   Moved by prophecy, as in this case, or by an inner prompting, the disciple sets out on his *quest* (vv.36f.). This is an opportunity which it is crucial to seize. The prompting must be obeyed. Commitment may not be postponed: it infers a positive response in the present:
    Today, if you hear his voice,
    Do not harden your hearts.   Ps. 95.7,8

2   Meeting Christ, the disciple is asked what he wants and replies with another question, 'Where are you staying?' (v.38). This is the *encounter*, in which the quest is clarified and the invitation is expressed (v.39a).

3   The disciple makes his *commitment* and stays where Christ 'stays' or 'abides'. As John 15.4ff. makes clear, the place where Christ abides is the Christian community, while the place where a Christian stays is in Christ. This is the only means of bearing fruit for him who is the true vine.

Andrew's first act was to go and find his brother Simon (v.41). This first exercise of apostleship, of missionary endeavour, gives Andrew a place of significance in this Gospel. Christians have been inspired by his example down the ages. The first priority for us all is evangelism, to bring the good news of Jesus Christ to others, especially to members of our own family. It would have been a less colourful early Christian community without Andrew's brother! But Andrew did not fail in his evangelistic task as a member of Christ. Jesus then foretells that his brother Simon will be called Cephas (Peter), the Rock (v.42).

The chain reaction from the Baptist's prophecy continues with the finding of Philip and Nathanael. Philip is mentioned in connection with Andrew in chapters 6 and 12, and so Andrew may also have found Philip, who in turn finds Nathanael. Nathanael is usually identified with Bartholomew who follows Philip in the synoptic lists of disciples.

The initial reluctance of Nathanael to believe Philip's message makes his affirmation an even more significant commitment. While Jesus' perception into the mind of Nathanael who had been meditating on the story of Jacob's ladder (Gen. 28.11–17, see Tuesday, Week 2) shows him to be the second Jacob, the true Israel in his own person, acknowledged by someone whom he had called a true Israelite, Nathanael.

Reflect on   (ref. v.48)

In the pragmatic thinking of the modern world, knowing something always means dominating something: 'Knowledge is power'. Through our scientific knowledge we acquire power over objects and can appropriate them.

For the Greek philosophers and the Fathers of the Church, knowing meant something different: it meant knowing in wonder. By knowing or perceiving, one participates in the life of the other. Here knowing does not transform the counterpart into the property of the knower; the knower does not appropriate what he knows. On the contrary, he is transformed through sympathy, becoming a participator in what he perceives. Knowledge confers fellowship.

Jürgen Moltmann, *The Trinity and the Kingdom of God*, p.9

Prayer

Eternal God, who art the light of the minds that know thee, the joy of the hearts that love thee, and the strength of the wills that serve thee: Grant us so to know thee that we may truly love thee, and so to love thee that we may fully serve thee, whom to serve is perfect freedom, in Jesus Christ our Lord.

After St Augustine (Parish Prayers, no. 1592)

The commitment of St Paul
2 CORINTHIANS 5.16—6.10

'Paul never wrote a more personal letter than 2 Corinthians . . . it would be equally true to say that he never wrote a more theological letter.' (C. K. Barrett, *The Second Epistle to the Corinthians*, p.32.) In this passage we see both the personal and the theological elements, mostly interwoven.

1 Becoming a Christian means a complete change of attitude, a different way of looking at things—and people. Being 'in Christ' (v.17) is the expression of our baptism, in which we shared the death and resurrection of Jesus. And one result of dying to the old self and living for Christ who died and rose again is that one is transfigured and shot through with, enfolded in, his glory. There is a shift of one's being from this age into the conditions of the world to come. 'In Christ is an expression of our Christian destiny. In him we are a new creation, the old has gone, the new has come!' For Paul this was both a personal experience and an objective, theological truth. The very experience of dying and living in Christ demonstrated the objective truth that the new creation was already taking over from the old.

2 Reconciliation is one of the great messages of Christianity. 'God was reconciling the world to himself in Christ' (v.19). The perfection of wholeness and unity in creation is being restored 'in Christ'. This message of reconciliation has now been entrusted to us so that we are now Christ's ambassadors (v.20). 'The proclamation of reconciliation is the service the church owes to the world.'

   An ambassador has the duty to speak out for his sovereign. For us Christians, if God is the great reconciler, that is our mission too. It may also be remarked that the term 'ambassador' is a very adequate description of Paul's own ministry. Fearlessly and frequently he spoke out as Christ's ambassador.

3 Christ's fearless ambassador was rewarded with the same hardships and rejection experienced by his Master. He was one of God's fellow-workers (6.1) and knew his great need of God's grace, if he was to endure to the end. He urges us to be recipients of this moment of salvation (v.2), and then proceeds to describe how he used God's grace.

In this autobiographical passage (vv.3–10) we discern the essential paradox of Christianity, so beautifully summarized in the final verses (vv.9 and 10). We are led to see how baptism and martyrdom can so easily become the two sides of the same coin. First he summarizes his external circumstances, the sufferings he endures for the sake of others (vv.4 and 5). Then he alludes to his spiritual and moral motives displayed in his work for Christ (v.6). (I incline to Barrett's view that this is not a reference to the Third Person of the Trinity but rather to the human spirit, 'holy' describing its ethical quality.)

In v.7 he looks at his work as a preacher. The truth of Paul's preaching is indicated by the manifestation of divine power that accompanies it. Constantly in his fearless proclamation of the gospel he found himself taken over by the Spirit, knowing that words had been given him which he had not meant to say. Perhaps this was why Jesus was so insistent that the preaching and healing should go together in the gospel proclamation. The combination of the two is a vehicle more likely to be used in the showing forth of God's power.

Finally he comes to the great Christian paradox, which is so consonant with the teaching of Jesus (e.g. Matt. 10.39). A sequence of double terms (v.8) leads naturally into the paradoxical quality of the Christian life (vv.9 and 10). Here we can feel the tension of life in the Kingdom, the 'not yet' and beyondness of eternal life constantly piercing into and illuminating life here and now. As Christians the 'now' will fill us with sorrow and lead us to realize our poverty. And yet, faith and hope tell us we are enfolded in a love so rich and fulfilling that we can at the same time experience joy and the knowledge we possess everything.

Reflect on
  Never let anything so fill you with sorrow that you forget the joy of Christ risen.
  Mother Teresa of Calcutta

Prayer
  Father, you have committed to men
    the good news of your saving love
  and set us as ambassadors for Christ
    in your world:

help us together to bear witness
to the message of reconciliation,
that in the life of your Church
men may become new creatures
in Jesus Christ our Lord.   Amen.
Collects with the New Lectionary

The commitment of the author of Hebrews
HEBREWS 11.1–16; 11.32—12.2

This eleventh chapter of Hebrews, which should obviously be read in full, is among the most eloquent passages in all literature. In the epistle it comes at the point where the writer has completed his theological argument setting forth the unique place and work of Jesus. He now feels enabled to express himself with complete freedom concerning the profound truths that have gripped him and to which he is so strongly committed.

'Faith is being sure of what we hope for and certain of what we do not see' (v.1). Here is the writer's definition of faith. It is God who gives us this certainty of commitment. But as we read on, we find that faith is so much more. It is the very gift that enables us to achieve the result of such commitment. Faith actually gives reality to our hopes, so that they may safely be accepted as the basis for our living and thinking. It gives us a certainty of the spiritual realm which, because of our upbringing in a scientific milieu, we find alien to our logical system of thought. Faith makes us certain of this spiritual realm, 'certain of what we do not see', leading us to perceive its deeper reality as the place where we are truly at home as God's children.

The first four men of faith mentioned here demonstrate some of the lasting qualities of commitment:

Abel. Here the principle is illustrated that the blood of the martyrs is the seed of the Church. 'By faith he still speaks, even though he is dead' (v.4). The influence of a good life leaves its mark on the life of the human race.

Enoch. In apocalyptic literature, Enoch underlines for us the fact that 'true faith means a penetration beyond the veil of sense and matter, which will give us a clue to the divine character' (Dr T. H. Robinson).

Noah. A perfect illustration of the necessity of taking God's word on trust. Such a commitment to the word of God inevitably stands out in sharp contrast to an unbelieving world.

Abraham. The real hero of faith (see Monday).

The great legacy of the Patriarchs is that they never wavered or faltered in their commitment of faith, nor did they ever doubt the fulfilment of their hopes. They had their spiritual eyes fixed on a *better* country (v.16—see passage below) and so 'God is not ashamed to be called their God', for he is 'not the God of the dead but of the living' (Matt. 22.32). In *him*, all men and women of faith still live on. They who are his, are his for ever.

From verse 32 onwards the writer contents himself with a summary and general statement, in which is described the suffering of the martyrs. It is an impressive record of faith's commitment, without which such sufferings could not have been borne. To them faith was indeed the reality of a *better* life. Even they, however, had to wait for its realization, wait for another generation, another era, upon which history had not yet dawned.

The whole procession of those men and women of faith culminates in the person and followers of Jesus Christ. The writer has before him the picture of an olympic stadium. The finishing tape is Jesus himself. The ranks of those who support and cheer on the contestants are these past heroes of faith (this 'cloud of witnesses'—12.1).

We ourselves are the contestants. The first part of our commitment is to 'throw off everything that hinders . . .', anything that may arise from the temptations of the world, the flesh and the devil. The second is not to divert our gaze from Jesus for a second, just as an athlete looks at nothing but the tape once he is under starter's orders. Jesus set his face like a flint (Isa. 50.7), 'for the joy set before him endured the cross, scorning its shame and sat down at the right hand of the throne of God' (12.2). That is why he is entitled to be called 'the author and perfector of our faith', the Alpha and Omega, the first and the last. The Christian life must be begun, continued and ended in Jesus Christ.

Reflect on

Wilfrid H. Bourne, commenting on the use of the word *better* in the letter to the Hebrews (see 11.4, 16 and 40) added: 'Life holds the most wonderful adventures for those who can face every mysterious change in their affairs with the question: "What better thing has God for me?" Such a self-query is not prompted by any selfish motive. We ought not to dismiss these attitudes as being the compensating qualities designed to tone disappointment into acceptance . . . We can put a splendid zest into [our commitment to] life when we turn from some apparent refusal and look for the "better way".'

Prayer

Lord Jesus, author and perfector of our faith,
you call your witnesses from every nation and era of history:
Make us thankful for their example and encouragement,
and strengthen us by their fellowship,
that like them, we may keep our gaze on you,
Our Lord and Saviour Jesus Christ.   Amen.

GROUP QUESTIONS

The adventure of commitment

1   What can Abraham's faith and spiritual experiences (Monday) teach us about the Christian life? (See Rom. 4.13–25.)

2   Jacob ends his vow (Gen. 28.22—Tuesday) by promising a tenth or tithe of all that God gives him. How seriously in this regard are we embarking on our own adventure of commitment?

3   What lessons which we have learned from pain and suffering have contributed to the good of the world around us? (Wednesday). And to our own good?

4   'Quest . . . encounter . . . commitment.' How true is this of our own discipleship? Have we seen our commitment as an adventure in knowing God? (Thursday)

5   'If anyone is in Christ, he is a new creation' (2 Cor. 5.17—Friday). Is the Church peopled by men and women of the new age? How can the Church help to prepare the world for the new age of the Kingdom? What signs, if any, has the new, emerging civilization in common with the new age of the Kingdom?

6   How much is a lack of commitment due to failure to keep our eyes on Jesus and to 'hear' and perceive the encouragement of the spiritual realm? (See Heb. 11.1—Saturday).

WEEK THREE

Read   Romans 8.26,27

Reflect on

Silence enables us to be aware of God, to let mind and imagination dwell upon his truth, to let prayer be listening before it is talking, and to discover our own selves in a way that is not always possible when we are making or listening to noise. There comes sometimes an interior silence in which the soul discovers itself in a new dimension of energy and peace, a dimension which the restless life can miss. If the possibilities of silence were often hard in biblical times they are infinitely harder in the world in which we live today. A world frightening in its speed and noise is a world where silence alone may enable man's true freedom to be found.

The ways in which meditation interpenetrates the praying of the Church and of the Christian are legion. A time of silence enables the Christian to share more deeply in the Church's sacramental worship. The Eucharist is the Church's central confrontation with the mystery of Christ, who died and rose again. By sharing in the Eucharist the Christian draws strength into his own time of silence, while the time of silence deepens what he brings and gives in the Eucharist. Into the Christian's use of silence there may flow the wonder of God the Creator, the recollection of the life and death and resurrection of Jesus, the recalling of scenes of his life, often a passage of the Bible, the glories of nature in which the finger of God is present, gratitude for personal blessings or the words of poets who tell of wonder and beauty. All these may stir meditation, and its course may be unpredictable.

Michael Ramsey, *Be still and know*, p.83f

Prayer

O Sabbath rest by Galilee!
    O calm of hills above,
Where Jesus knelt to share with thee
The silence of eternity,
    Interpreted by love!

Drop thy still dews of quietness,
    Till all our strivings cease;

Take from our souls the strain and stress,
And let our ordered lives confess
    The beauty of thy peace.
J. G. Whittier

The Adventure of Praying

A Psalm of David
PSALM 23

During his pastoral visit to Britain, Pope John Paul II gave an address on education at St Andrew's College, Bearsden, in Scotland. The students responded in song. He thanked them, saying that singing was an important part of college life. As he left they sang again—'Will ye no come back again?' He did—despite the efforts of his attendants to hurry him on! Gaining the microphone he said: 'My brother bishops are saying it is very important in the Church to pray. It is doubly important to sing.'

Music has its own therapy, as King David knew full well. The sweet Psalmist of Israel constantly reverted to song (and on one occasion to dance) when he wished to communicate with his God.

The twenty-third Psalm is the most loved and sung of all David's songs. The reasons are not hard to see. The Lord is the subject of the poem; his name is mentioned as the first and last word. In between, his activity is listed in seven ways: 'he makes', 'he leads' (v.2), 'he restores', 'he guides' (v.3), 'you are with me' (v.4), 'you prepare a table', 'you anoint my head' (v.5). The whole psalm is focused on the Lord, whose compassion, constant vigilance and ceaseless presence give to life a richness and colour that can only issue in song.

The dominant theme is that of God as protector and guide. The poem opens using pastoral imagery to describe the loving care of the Lord. He is 'my shepherd' (v.1) who gives me rich pasturage and leads me by restful waters (v.2), in paths of righteousness (v.3), bringing serenity and security to life. The fact that the Psalmist calls him '*my* shepherd' underlines the bond of affection that binds him to his Lord. Undoubtedly this personal element has made it one of the best loved and most intimate prayers of any religion.

These bonds between the sheep and shepherd, the believer and his Lord, will one day undergo the test of suffering, 'the valley of the shadow of death' (v.4). The Lord's presence and care even in such an extremity will, however, banish all anxiety. It is at this point the pronoun changes from the third to the more intimate second person: '*you* are with me; *your* rod and staff, they comfort me' (v.4). Having spoken *about* the Lord, he now speaks directly *to* the Lord.

The imagery changes in the last two verses to that of hospitality. David sees the Lord, in his generosity, as the perfect host, who prepares the table, anoints him with oil and fills his cup to overflowing. Such fullness leads to the finality of an unlimited relationship with the Lord for the whole of life: 'I will dwell in the house of the Lord for ever' (v.6). A secure present leads to an assured future.

For a Christian, the imagery of this beautiful song is deeply significant. It is Jesus who is the Good Shepherd (John 10.11) and also the Christ, the Lord's anointed. As the anointed of God, he anoints his children in baptism and in the anointing of the sick. As the Host in the Eucharist who prepares the table, he feeds his sheep and fills the cup to the brim.

A recipient of such generous compassion and constant care for his/her spiritual, physical and mental well-being can only resonate to the song the Creator is eternally singing, which is another way of chanting, 'I will dwell in the house of the Lord for ever'.

Reflect on
Jesus said, 'I am the good shepherd; I know my sheep and my sheep know me—just as the Father knows me and I know the Father—and I lay down my life for the sheep.

'I have other sheep that are not of this sheep pen. I must bring them also. They too will listen to my voice, and there shall be one flock and one shepherd.'
John 10.14–16

Prayer
God of peace,
who brought again from the dead
     our Lord Jesus Christ,
that great shepherd of the sheep,
by the blood of the eternal covenant:
make us perfect in every good work to do your will,
and work in us that which is well-pleasing
     in your sight;
through Jesus Christ our Lord.   Amen.
Collect for Easter 2 (ASB)

Elijah's meditation
1 KINGS 19.1–18

Charles de Foucauld, the founder of the Little Brothers of Jesus and a holy man of the desert, used to live in a rectangular sort of hut. At one end was a box which served as his altar, upon which was laid the open Bible. At the other, there were no doors: it was open to the world and therefore to anyone who wanted to enter.

Elijah was a man of the desert who had the same openness to his God and to the world. At this stage, as so often happens with us, the burdens of the world had pressed upon him and taken their toll. After his victory for the Lord on Carmel, his life came under threat from the wicked Jezebel. He was afraid and fled (v.3), and leaving his servant he went on alone into the desert (v.4).

1 *His first prayer came from the heart.* Alone with his Lord in the desert the truth came out: 'I have had enough, Lord' (v.4). The end of one's tether is a spiritually creative point to reach! And 'Lord, I'm out of my depth', is an utterance and moment of truth in the spiritual life. It is just at that point, perhaps only at that point, when we cease to struggle on in our own strength, that the Lord can fully enter the situation and come to our aid.

2 The experience of David (see yesterday) who found *an endless generosity in the Lord's hospitality*, was now to enter Elijah's consciousness: 'Get up and eat,' twice repeated, 'for the journey is too much for you' (v.7). Is this our own sacramental experience? Do we get up and eat and drink (at the Eucharist) realizing we shall be 'strengthened by that food' for our pilgrimage? (v.8).

3 The first encounter on Horeb, 'What are you doing here, Elijah?' (v.9) seems a little odd, if he had been sent there. But *self-examination is a necessary prelude* to prayerful discourse with the Lord. Elijah rattles off his explanation (v.10), almost in one breath, just as we sometimes rattle through the confession. The reply ignores the explanation and so lifts Elijah from his preoccupation with his earthly chores to a readiness to contemplate his Lord: 'Go out and stand on the mountain in the presence of the Lord' (v.11).

4 *An alertness to the Lord's presence* lies at the heart of *contemplative prayer.* Would the Lord be in the powerful wind

or the earthquake (v.11) or the fire? (v.12). He might have been, for he can use any phenomenon as a vehicle of his presence. But in this case it was 'a gentle whisper' (v.12). The contemplative has to learn how to be still and how to be silent so that even a sound of gentle stillness can be discerned and the Lord's voice heard.

5   Only after all the preliminaries of prayer, and a meaningful experience of the silence and the stillness, is the instruction of the Lord heard and his will discerned. As George Bennett used to say, we begin praying when we cease to pray! It was in *the silent afterglow* of his disclosure moment that Elijah found the answer to the burden with which he came: Hazael, Jehu and Elisha are to be the next generation of leaders and there are seven thousand who have remained loyal to the true God. It was a message heard on 'the other side of silence'.

Reflect on

If chosen souls could never be alone,
In deep mid-silence, open-doored to God,
No greatness ever had been dreamed or done.
James Russell Lowell

Prayer

Almighty God and Father, help us to be still in your presence, that we may know ourselves to be your people, and you to be our God; through Jesus Christ our Lord.   Amen.
James M. Todd

The prayer of Nehemiah
NEHEMIAH 1.1—2.6

Do you recall receiving any particularly distressing news and the impact it made on you? The death of a dear one, a major accident, a stunning disappointment or hearing of some unspeakable suffering that so many men and women have endured this century? Think for a moment. Can you still feel the pain? To a Jew, Jerusalem ('city of peace') was God's own sanctuary. The supreme tragedy would be if its walls were broken down and the Temple destroyed. This was the news Nehemiah heard, as told in Ezra 4.7–23. He broke down and wept and poured out himself (v.4) before the Lord, to whom he turned for everything, quite naturally. We need not go into the problems of the Ezra–Nehemiah documents. Suffice it to say that this story of Nehemiah is straightforward and bears the stamp of genuine autobiography. It speaks of Nehemiah's dependence on God, to whom he frequently resorted in prayer. And his prayer, especially in this case, was intense, concentrated—'for some days I mourned and fasted and prayed before the God of heaven'.

It led Nehemiah into a great adventure—the rebuilding of Jerusalem of which he was elected Governor and was able to overcome the stormy opposition of Sanballat (chapter 4). This prayer also showed that formal prayer in Nehemiah's life spilled over into a constant lifting of the heart to his Lord. In fact prayer became his life and his life became prayer. Let us pray through his prayer:

1 *The greatness of God* (1.5). An immediate lifting of our hearts heavenward, to the Father Creator who loves and is love. Our response: loving obedience to his promptings.

2 *The constancy of prayer* for a particular request (1.6a). Day and night. Such constancy evolved into the seven offices of the religious life. We see it again in the increasing number of prayer vigils. Jesus rose 'a great while before day' to be with his heavenly Father.

3 *The confession of sin* (1.6b,7). Prayer is a relationship and everything that sours that relationship and comes between God and us has to be confessed. It is a corporate confession (we are part of the society we live in and are part of its sin) and also a personal confession (full confession of our private sins must also be made).

4   *The mercy of God* (1.8,9). Faithfulness in man reflects the faithfulness and mercy of God, which is limitless. God will go to 'the farthest horizon' to gather his people, so great is the power of his redeeming love: his mighty hand is always stretched out to heal (1.10).

5   *Prayer issues in action* (1.11). He ends with a strong plea for God to answer his prayer *today*, for he goes in the strength of his prayer with God to do what he has prayed through and been prompted to do. It is our willingness to step out into God's will in his strength *today* that will bring the colour and adventure into our life. What's holding you back? 'I will go forth in the strength of the Lord God . . .'

Reflect on

All our power for good is derived from God. From God, I say; for he is the source of our life and our strength; from him we gain vitality so that in our present position we recognize beforehand the signs of things that are to come. Only let fear be the guardian of innocence, so that the Lord, who in his kindness has streamed into our minds with the inflowing of his heavenly mercy, may through righteous activity be retained as a guest of the soul that delights in him, lest the security we have received should produce heedlessness and the old enemy creep in unawares once more.

Cyprian (Bishop of Carthage, 248–258), *Ad Donatum*, 4

Prayer

Lord, let your ear be attentive to the prayer of your servant,
    and to the prayer of all your servants who revere your name:
Give your servant success today in all things I attempt in your
    name and for your glory.   Amen.

Jesus' teaching on prayer
LUKE 11.1–13

Prayer has a special place in Luke's Gospel. Here he shows how it was a main theme in Jesus' instruction of his disciples. This section, which is an exhortation to prayer, falls into four parts:

1   A request for instruction on how to pray, to which a pattern of prayer is given (vv.1–4). It was Jesus' own example of prayer which elicited the request (v.1). In return he offers them a pattern for prayer we now know as the Lord's Prayer. We note its shortened form which is probably original (vv.2–4).

    It may be, because of the reference to John the Baptist, that the disciples, who presumably prayed already, were asking for a distinctive prayer for their own movement or group, by which they would be known as the followers of Jesus. If so, then perhaps this could well be called the prayer of the Kingdom, following the main thrust of Jesus' message and teaching. The opening part may well have been based on the Jewish Qaddish prayer which includes the petition: 'May he let his kingdom rule in your lifetime and in your day and in the lifetime of the whole house of Israel, speedily and soon.' The same note of urgency is sounded in the first two requests of the Lord's Prayer, which ask for the establishment of God's purposes on a cosmic scale: hallowed be your name, your kingdom come (v.2).

    The significant addition is the opening word 'Father', the simple form 'Abba' used by Jesus in his own prayer. In teaching the disciples to use this form of address Jesus clearly wanted them to share the same close relationship he himself enjoyed with the heavenly Father. This is the relationship he wants us to enjoy too, while in our prayer for the coming of the Kingdom, we can rejoice that in Jesus and through 'the power of his resurrection and the fellowship of sharing in his sufferings' (Phil. 3.10), God's kingly rule (i.e. Kingdom) is already breaking into this world on a cosmic scale.

    The remaining half of the prayer details the three personal needs of the disciples: a daily supply of spiritual and physical nourishment (v.3), a new relationship of reconciliation with the Father and their fellow human beings, and his power to preserve them in time of temptation (v.4). The very fact of these needs should surely increase our longing for the Kingdom.

2   A parable showing God's readiness to hear prayer (vv.5–8). This seems to be the original intention of Jesus' teaching, for as in the parable of the unjust judge, the unwillingness of the householder is by implication contrasted with God's willingness to answer prayer.

Another interpretation, possibly equally valid, is to see the parable as an encouragement to persist in prayer, to go on praying even when an immediate answer is apparently not forthcoming. Both interpretations bring us the true teaching of Jesus.

3   A statement on the certainty that God will answer prayer (vv.9 and 10; compare with Matthew 7.7–11). Three different phrases are used, concerned with asking, seeking and knocking, and should all be taken as applying to prayer. The tenses in verse 10 are different, present and future. It is not right to place a timescale on our requests: all we know is that God will answer our prayer (and Jesus here gives us this assurance) *at the right time*—that is, in *his* time.

4   The assurance that God will answer prayer even more readily than a human father responding to his children's requests (vv.11–13). Jesus asserts this truth followed by an even more significant truth: the heavenly Father's gifts are of a spiritual order. He will 'give the Holy Spirit to those who ask him' (v.13). With such an encouragement, how frequently and persistently could we knock and seek and ask the heavenly Father for the gift of the Holy Spirit! How perfectly would our daily needs then be supplied. Should we not resolve to ask for this gift of the Spirit, daily, many times a day? 'Ask and it will be given to you . . .' (vv.9 and 10).

Reflect on
Again, I tell you that if two of you on earth agree about anything you ask for, it will be done for you by my Father in heaven. For where two or three come together in my name, there am I with them.
Matthew 18.19,20

Prayer

Father, lead me to someone (today),
with whom I may join in prayer
in your Son's name,
and in his presence.   Amen.

Jesus' own prayer
JOHN 17

It is appropriate that we should read and ponder this chapter on a Friday, the day on which Christ died. It has been called the High Priestly prayer, but Bishop Michael Ramsey (in *Be still and know*, p.47) suggests a better title might be the Prayer of Consecration, 'for at its centre Jesus consecrates himself to his death on behalf of the disciples'. Its context is the approaching cross and passion of Jesus on that Good Friday; it therefore forms the prelude to the death of Jesus.

The cross in the fourth Gospel is viewed as the glorification of Jesus. It is not surprising that glory is the theme of this prayer: the passion and the completion of Jesus' work is seen as the means of giving glory to Father and Son (vv.1 and 4), reflecting the timeless sharing of glory from eternity (vv.5 and 24); the disciples give glory to Jesus (v.10) and the glory enables, and is reflected by, the unity of the converts and the disciples (v.22). The prayer divides into three parts:

1 Concerning Jesus himself (vv.1–5). At the beginning of his ministry, Jesus came proclaiming 'the time has come, the Kingdom of God is near' (Mark 1.15). So now at its close he repeats these prophetic words, 'Father, the time has come. Glorify your Son, that your Son may glorify you' (v.1). The Kingdom of heaven was opened to all believers once the sharpness of death was overcome; then Jesus could take his place at the Father's right hand in glory. From this 'position' of exaltation he could give gifts to mankind (see Eph. 4.7ff), especially 'eternal life' (vv.2 and 3), the life of the Kingdom which brought the knowledge of God.

Lord, grant me to know you more deeply today, and see your glory more clearly.

2 Concerning the disciples (vv.6–19). The glory Jesus gave the Father on earth by completing his work (v.4) included making known the Father to the disciples, who have received and obeyed the revelation (vv.6–8). It is for them he now prays (vv.9–19),
> that they may be protected 'by the power of your name' (v.11),
> that they may be one (v.11),

that they may be possessed of the full joy of Jesus (v.13),
that they may be protected from the evil one (v.15),
that they may be sanctified, consecrated, by the truth (v.17).

Lord, may I apply these words of prayer to myself, and so realize that for me you consecrated yourself.

3 Concerning those who will believe through the disciples' testimony (vv.20–6). The keynote of this final section is unity and has constantly inspired the ecumenical movement. Jesus prayed 'that all of them may be one'. And this unity has not merely a horizontal dimension, but also a vertical dimension because the unity we are to experience is that within the blessed Trinity, a unity that resembles the Father's oneness in the Son and the Son's oneness in the Father. We are to find our unity in God alone and that for two reasons: 'that the world may believe that you have sent me' and that 'you have loved them even as you have loved me' (vv.21–3).

The prayer then moves towards heaven, praying that all may be with Jesus and see the vision of his eternal glory (v.24); and back to earth, praying that while they remain as 'a presence' in an unbelieving world, they may be kept in the Father's love for Jesus and through the presence of Jesus in them (vv.25 and 26).

Lord Jesus, as you drew your power to pray from the Father,
So may we receive the power to pray from heaven
Where you reign in the glory of the Father.   Amen.

Reflect on

the three parts of the Prayer, using the petitions at the end of each section.

Prayer

Take my life, and let it be
Consecrated, Lord, to thee;
Take my moments and my days,
Let them flow in ceaseless praise.

Take my will, and make it thine;
It shall be no longer mine,
Take my heart; it is thine own:
It shall be thy royal throne.

Take my love; my Lord, I pour
At thy feet its treasure-store.
Take myself, and I will be
Ever, only, all for thee.   Amen.
Frances R. Havergal

A prayer of the first Christians
ACTS 4.13–31

Luke was not only a doctor and historian: he was also a theologian and teacher. In telling the story of the lame man who was healed at the temple gate called Beautiful, he had a purpose. That purpose was to show how obedient those early Christians were to Jesus' command to his disciples (see Luke 9.2 and 10.9) to proclaim the good news both by preaching and healing.

In order to do this, he spreads the story over two whole chapters in Acts 3 and 4. First we have the healing (3.1–10) followed by Peter's first preachment (3.12–26). The disciples were then arrested by the temple guard and jailed (4.1–4). Their appearance before the rulers and elders the next day gave Peter an opportunity for a second preachment in which he didn't mince his words (4.5–12; note v.10).

At this point our reading takes up the story. Peter and John may have lacked education and belonged to the working class, but the fact that they had been with Jesus altered everything (v.13). The presence of the lame man now *healed* was also a powerful witness that changed the situation (v.14). All the rulers felt able to do was to warn the disciples not to speak in this name again (vv.15–18). Peter's reply to this was quite predictable and very much to the point (vv.19 and 20). But no more could be said because 'all the people were praising God for what had happened' (v.21).

Now they return to where their colleagues are gathered (in a vigil of prayer?) and after recounting all that has happened they turn to prayer. They praise the Creator (v.24) who spoke by the Holy Spirit in a prophetic word about the opposition they would encounter (vv.25 and 26). How that has come true! (vv.27 and 28).

So they come boldly to the throne of grace and make a three-fold request, which we could well adopt as a pattern for our own daily prayer for our health and salvation (vv.29 and 30):

Lord, consider their threats. All that is against us in life, our anxieties and troubles, our problems and suffering, has to be brought to the Lord, to the foot of the cross, surrendered and *left there*. It is the prayer of resignation: 'Lord, I can't cope, it's now over to you.' It is only at this point that the Lord can enter the situation in his almighty power.

Enable your servants to speak your word with great boldness. They could have asked for anything—peace, security, safety, immunity from persecution. But they knew they had been sent (apostled) by Christ on his mission. There was no turning back once one had put one's hand to the plough (Luke 9.62). So they asked for *boldness*, a continuing source of supply of that characteristic already noted in them by the rulers (v.13), which was a direct result of being in the presence of Jesus. Perhaps our timidity and fearfulness in Christ's service say something about the small portion of time we spend consciously in his presence. Let us approach the throne of grace with boldness and ask continually for this gift (see Heb. 4.16).

Stretch out your hand to heal . . . through the name of your holy servant Jesus. The 'mighty hand and outstretched arm' (see Psalm 136.10–15) which effected the Exodus and which has now raised Jesus from the dead, is still effective in all its timeless potency to heal. How the world would be transfigured if we believed this to be true! Let us pray for a like obedience and boldness to that of the early Christians, which will put us again in the way of his outstretched hand and mighty power.

Reflect on

The Gospel is not only a programme for action, it is also a proclamation of the power at our disposal . . . As pastors, we need to learn how to use Christ's healing power, or how to be instruments enabling him to exercise that power on one another . . . Christ came not only to proclaim a message, but to use a healing power . . . His healing brings happiness and freedom.

Cardinal Basil Hume, OSB, *Searching for God*, p.171

Prayer

Use verses 29 and 30 of Acts 4.

GROUP QUESTIONS

The adventure of praying

1 How much of our praying is *about* the Lord and how much is *to* the Lord? (Monday). What has David's faith to teach us?

2 How much are solitude, stillness and silence part of our own venture of prayer? (Tuesday)

3 'Abba', 'Father', shows Jesus' own special relationship to God. 'He spoke to God as a child to its father: confidently and securely, and yet at the same time reverently and obediently.' (Joachim Jeremias) How far do we see our praying as a forging of this ever deepening relationship? (Thursday)

4 What does Jesus' prayer (Friday) teach us about our own adventure in praying and consecrating ourselves to his service?

5 How far does the healing dimension to our faith make the adventure of preaching and praying more powerful and effective? (Saturday)

6 How many of our present problems, anxieties, etc. have we actually surrendered to the Lord? If we were actually granted our prayer for boldness, what difference would it make to our Christian adventure personally, as a group, as a church?

WEEK FOUR

Read   Psalm 123.1 and 2

Reflect on

This looking to God is contemplation. It is an inward gaze into the depths of the soul and, for that very reason, beyond the soul to God. The more the soul finds God, the more it forgets itself and yet finds itself in God. It is an unwavering 'gaze', where 'looking' is always 'hearing'; for what is looked at is the free and infinite Person who, from the depths of his freedom, is able to give himself in a manner ever new, unexpected and unpredictable . . .

This gaze, this 'looking', is directed towards the perfect fulfilment promised to created nature in its entirety. In seeing and hearing God, it experiences the highest joy, that of being fulfilled in itself, but fulfilled by something infinitely greater than itself and, for that very reason, completely fulfilled and made blessed . . .

In every age, contemplation, as 'vision' of divine truth, has been looked on, in the Church, as a kind of foretaste of the eternal blessedness to come. The difference, however, is only a relative one. In eternity too God, in his supremely free self-giving, will not cease to be our fulfilment and so will we, while beholding God, not cease to hang on his lips and be hearers.

Hans Urs von Balthasar, *Prayer*, pp.20f.

Prayer

Divine Saviour, I surrender my heart wholly to thee for ever. Kindle there a fire of love whence shall arise like incense a ceaseless prayer to Heaven bringing down to me a ceaseless stream of graces. Thy heart, O my God, is ever concerned with me, and is it not therefore right that my heart should be concerned with thee; O perfect Beauty, infinite Goodness, how couldst thou be less interesting to me than I to thee? Thy delight is with the children of men, to converse with them and shall I not delight to converse with thee? Continual love and continual adoration are the portion of the blessed; why should I not make them my portion on earth, my foretaste of celestial joy? Shall I always be your enemy, always oppose my true happiness? No, indeed. I will begin to pray to thee, my God, in this life, that I may continue my prayer throughout eternity.   Amen.

Jean-Nicolas Grou, SJ, *How to Pray*, pp.87f

The Adventure of Loving

Jacob's adventure
GENESIS 29.1–30

After Jacob made his commitment at Bethel (see Tuesday in Week 2), he continued his journey eastwards (v.1). It was a mission he had been sent on by his father Isaac, in order to find a wife from his mother Rebekah's kindred. So he was wending his way to Paddan Aram, to the house of his maternal grandfather, Bethuel, to take a wife from among his first cousins, the daughters of Laban (Gen. 28.2).

On his arrival in the country, he meets some shepherds and from their conversation finds out all he needs to know (vv.2–8). But the special blessing he had received at Bethel was immediately apparent in that, even while he was speaking, Rachel, Laban's younger daughter, arrived with her father's sheep (v.9). The instant attraction he felt for her inspired him to a feat of gallantry in defiance of local custom (v.10) and then he embraced her (v.11).

We must remember that the writer is in fact recording the origins of the twelve tribes of Israel, and already we can discern the hand of the Lord, guiding the destiny of his people: Isaac gives Jacob a blessing and sends him on his mission of love; Jacob receives the Lord's blessing at Bethel and is promised a great inheritance; at once he is led to his mother's kindred of whom the first person he meets is to become the love of his life and the mother of his favourite sons, Joseph and Benjamin. Israel's election comes solely through the grace of God: that is the message the writer wants to be heard, loud and clear.

It was also born of true love, as far as Jacob was concerned. He readily agreed to stay and work for Laban, requesting that his wages, for seven years' work, should be the hand of Rachel with whom he was in love. And those long years 'seemed like only a few days to him because of his love for her' (vv.15–20).

But even the grace of God can encounter difficulties! Even such love finds obstacles in its path. Laban tricked Jacob (not for the last time) on his wedding day and gave him Leah the 'weak-eyed' elder daughter. And though he relented and gave him Rachel soon afterwards he gained another seven years of labour out of Jacob through this sordid deal.

We conclude therefore that the senior ones among the tribal patriarchs were born out of family tension, as their names indicate: Reuben=(the Lord) has looked on my affliction; Simeon=(the Lord) has heard; Levi=(my husband) will be joined; and as life becomes more bearable for deceiver and deceived—Judah=I will praise.

And yet—and this is one of the great lessons of the Jacob/Joseph saga in the Old Testament, indeed of life itself—out of adversity and disharmony God can weave a pattern of good. That is the wonder of his grace and power: he is the God who can ever bring good from ill, a process that finds its zenith in the cross of Jesus.

So here we find that even out of this mean trickery practised on Jacob (he had played a few tricks himself on his brother Esau in his younger days!), there came forth the beginnings of God's chosen race, a mighty people through whom he would work his will, from whose stock his only-begotten son would be born, a race that still has its own peculiar contribution to make to salvation history in God's final purpose; while among those first sons of dissension were born the two patriarchs of the royal Messianic and priestly tribes of Israel.

The message must surely be: the grace of God knows no bounds and true love does triumph—in the end.

Reflect on   Ephesians 3.14–21

Prayer

O God, who hast prepared for them that love thee
such good things as pass man's understanding:
Pour into our hearts such love towards thee,
that we, loving thee above all things (and in all things),
may obtain thy promises,
which exceed all that we can desire;
through Jesus Christ our Lord.   Amen.
Trinity 6, BCP
(the fuller version is used at the Burrswood healing services)

Hosea's problem marriage and its reconciliation
HOSEA 1 & 3

Hosea was one of the prophetic voices of the 8th century BC. Like Amos he spoke mainly to Israel, because her end was nearer. But he also spoke to Judah because her turn would come. He dated his message by the kings of both kingdoms (v.1).

His name itself was prophetic: Hosea is a variant of Joshua, from which the name 'Jesus' also comes, and means 'Jahweh saves'. This is also a statement of personal experience, for knowing God as a Person was important to Hosea and, because of this and his teaching on love, he has been called the St John of the Old Testament. He was a prophet of hope despite his warnings of judgement to come.

There have been various interpretations of these two chapters in an effort to assess the relationship of Hosea's public ministry to his private life. So J. B. Phillips comments (in *Four Prophets*, 1963): 'It is not always clear whether the prophet's experience with Gomer is teaching him about God, or whether he is learning about his wife from his understanding of Israel. The two run on parallel lines and flash a meaning across to each other.'

As regards the content of the two chapters it seems that Hosea took a wife, Gomer, at the Lord's bidding, who bore him three children to whom Hosea gave prophetic names. Gomer was later unfaithful to him, an experience that however increased his knowledge of God, and sometime after that (chapter 3) he reclaimed her, again at the Lord's bidding, buying her back from the man she was living with and vowing from then on mutual faithfulness. We might summarize the passage thus: 'A simple historical record of obedience to God which resulted not only in a broken marriage which was restored, but in a prophecy which speaks the truth in love'. (J. B. Hindley).

Marriage is the model frequently used in the Old Testament for the relationship between Jahweh and his people. Adultery is therefore the sin of forsaking him and turning to other gods (v.2). In obedience Hosea acts out a parallel experience (v.3).

The important factor is the birth of their three children who are given prophetic names, as were the sons of Isaiah (Isa. 7.3; 8.3):

Jezreel—'God sows' (v.4). Jezreel was in fact a fertile valley now desecrated by Jehu's massacre, who though acting in obedience to Elijah's word (see Tuesday in Week 3), had not sought first and foremost to do the Lord's will.

Lo-Ruhamah (a daughter)—'not loved' (vv.6 and 7). The message is that, because of Israel's unfaithfulness, God will withdraw his love, while still maintaining his love for Judah whose salvation by God alone is foretold.

Lo-Ammi—'not my people' (v.9). Despite disowning his people, God has a plan of ultimate salvation and the chapter ends on a message of hope: they will be called 'sons of the living God' and 'will be reunited' (vv.10 and 11).

This reunion is fulfilled in Hosea's own life as described in chapter 3. He had learned the human loves in his earlier experience, affection for people (including sexual attraction) and pity for the helpless. Now he was to learn the experience of covenant-love (*hesed*), the love God felt for his people, steadfast love, which included mercy and forgiveness, gentleness and strength, zeal and perseverance.

This perfect love of God, shown in 'his blessings in the last days' (v.5), when he sent his only begotten Son 'for us men and for our salvation', was now to be glimpsed by Hosea in his act of reconciliation with his wife and their vow of mutual love and faithfulness. Hosea's legacy to religious consciousness was a deeper and wider understanding of the God who is love.

Reflect on

> My song is love unknown,
>   My Saviour's love to me,
> Love to the loveless shown,
>   That they might lovely be.
>   O who am I,
>   That for my sake
>   My Lord should take
>   Frail flesh and die?

Samuel Crossman

Prayer

Lord, since I truly believe that Thy loving, guiding hand is upon my life, help me to be sensitive to every guiding pressure. Amen.

Leslie D. Weatherhead

Love's full extent
JOHN 13.1–17

The writer of the Fourth Gospel begins his account of the feet-washing with an emphatic reference to the time (see Friday in Week 3) and the explanation that this is a demonstration of Jesus' love for his disciples in its fullest extent (v.1).

'The time had come for him to leave this world.' Jesus was always very conscious of 'the hour', the time appointed by his Father. The New Testament word for 'time' does in fact mean opportunity, the right time and so God's time (e.g. Rom. 13.11). It is a consciousness we have tended to lose since we have been ruled by clock time. For Jesus, 'the right time' was important; it ought to be for his followers.

'The full extent of his love.' The direct example of his love followed in the feet-washing, but it was symbolic of the attitude of selfless love that will permeate the body of his followers when he is in the midst and also pointed to the cross, the occasion and symbol of the greatest demonstration of love the world has ever known. Here, writ large, was love's fullest extent (cf. John 15.12f.; 1 John 4.10). This first verse, therefore, introduces not only the supper, but the whole passion. Because of the connection of baptism with Jesus' passion and death, it is worthy of note that Jesus demonstrates his love by a *washing* of the disciples.

Jesus' preparation for this act underlines his deep humility. He knew 'the Father had put all things under his power' (v.3), and yet of all things he could have claimed he chose a towel (v.4), the symbol of service (cf. Luke 22.27). This episode is the perfect demonstration of the virtue Jesus made his own, which reached its climax on the cross. (It may be remarked here that while the Synoptists all record the Last Supper, this writer substitutes the feet-washing; both actions point to the cross.)

The episode with Peter (vv.6–10) is a lovely piece of writing and seemingly so characteristic of Jesus' chief disciple, always ready to take a lead and have his say. The great lesson Peter learns in this encounter is that there is a generosity in receiving that sometimes exceeds that in giving. Pride has first to be broken down, so that it becomes a trenchant lesson in humility. The lesson will be driven home when the Master he has betrayed actually dies for him. Paradoxically this is the moment of hope and resurrection. And that is why the disciples are clean (v.10).

The remainder of the passage (vv.12–17) is an explanation to the disciples of the practical significance of his action. In their mission they must follow the Master's example. But the symbolic significance is only just below the surface. Jesus had in fact made a revolutionary inroad into the realm of human relationships. This episode is a practical application of the Magnificat philosophy (cf. Luke 1.53f.). The spirit of Christ is one of humble service to the world and this action of love at its full extent has to begin within the Church (v.14). Too often the Lord is betrayed in the house of his friends in this regard (cf. Zech. 13.6), but 'anyone who does not love his brother, whom he has seen, cannot love God, whom he has not seen' (1 John 4.20).

The test of our generosity and of our love could be whether we are going to permit our Lord and Teacher (v.14) to wash our feet, and if so, when—and how.

Reflect on

All emotions hostile to Thy will, and therefore to my welfare, are being dissolved and washed out of my deep mind by the inflowing of Thy cleansing and renewing love.

Leslie Weatherhead, *Private House of Prayer*

Prayer

Jesus Lord and Master, who served your disciples in washing their feet: serve us often, serve us daily, in washing our motives, our ambitions, our actions; that we may share with you in your mission to the world and serve others gladly for your sake; to whom be glory for ever.   Amen.

based on *The Christian Priest Today* by Michael Ramsey

A description of love
1 CORINTHIANS 13

Again we come to one of the great pieces of literature, which has a rhythmic beauty all its own. But this beauty must not blind us to the perceptive truths about love which the apostle unfolds for us. The German theologian Harnack declared this hymn of praise to be 'the greatest, strongest, deepest thing Paul ever wrote'. The love of God for the undeserving, this totally giving love (*agapē*), is what Hosea glimpsed in his experience of love (see Tuesday).

Paul's treatment of the theme falls into three parts:

1 Spiritual gifts without love are of no use to their possessor (vv.1–3). Natural eloquence and even the gift of tongues can be mere noise and unhelpful without love for those present. Intellectualism, prophecy and philanthropy can also be counterproductive without love. In these verses, 'I' is still in the centre of the picture, 'If I speak', 'If I have the gift', 'If I give . . .'

2 The characteristics of God-like and selfless love (vv.4–7). Each description is integral to the whole which is perfection (v.10).

   Patient—having power to avenge and yet not doing so. The word (*makrothumein* in Greek) is used of God's forbearance with us.

   Kind—not weakness, but active generosity and helpfulness.

   Does not envy the success, the gifts or the possessions of others.

   Does not boast—love has a self-effacing quality, as seen in Jesus.

   Is not proud—arrogance is mere self-inflation, alienating others.

   Is not rude—courtesy, tact, politeness may be lesser virtues but they make greater human beings.

   Is not self-seeking—Solzhenitsyn, commenting on life in the West, said he heard people talking more about their rights than their obligations! It is hard for love to dwell in an acquisitive society.

   Is not easily angered—exasperation with people or things is more a comment on oneself than on them.

Keeps no record of wrongs—brooding over wrongs and nursing resentments shows a lack of love and forgiveness. It is also a recipe for ill-health!

Does not delight in evil but rejoices in the truth—enjoyment of gossip and derogatory talk about others is a sad trait of human nature. Christian love rather rejoices in the good and true facts about others and in their success.

Always protects, always trusts, always hopes, always perseveres—the last of these words (Greek—*hypomenein*) is one of the greatest words of the New Testament and virtually includes the others. It is the steadfast endurance under trial, in which an entirely trustful hope and invincible joy are displayed.

3 In the third part (vv.8–13), Paul stresses three points:

   a The permanency of love (v.8). Compare with the Song of Songs 8.7:
   'Many waters cannot quench love;
   rivers cannot wash it away.'

   b The wholeness of love (vv.9–12). Corinth was famous (amongst other things) for its manufacture of mirrors, made of highly polished metal. At their best they gave only an imperfect reflection. This world is full of puzzling reflections, but the day will come when new knowledge and love, even our very being, will be whole. We shall become the perfection God intended us to be, a true reflection of himself, who is love.

   c The supremacy of love (v.13). There is a unity about these three, sometimes called the theological virtues. They also have permanency. The definite article comes before the final mention of love, the only instance. Perhaps this makes a clear reference to *the* love of God himself, which has obvious supremacy.

Reflect on

If you will be like him, be humble and loving. And charity means that you must have a true love for your fellow-Christians.

Walter Hilton in *The Ladder of Perfection*

Prayer

My God,
I believe in thee: increase my faith.
I hope in thee: strengthen my hope.
I love thee, and desire to love thee more and more,
    and above all things,
    and all others for thee:
quicken my love and make me wholly thine.   Amen.

from *Daily Prayer and Praise*, compiled by George Appleton

The power of love
ROMANS 5.1–8; 8.35–9

Paul has been dealing in great themes: Romans is a majestic canvas. Righteousness, judgement and justification have been painted in the brightest colours so far. Justification is 'the result of God's gracious act of redemption in Jesus Christ'.

Now he can paint in some of the other colours that flow from this:

peace with God (v.1), the great Easter gift and salutation;

access (by faith into this grace, v.2), one of Paul's great words, see Ephesians 2.18 and 3.12;

a new joy, both 'in the *hope* of the *glory* of God' (v.2) and 'in our sufferings' (v.3), for both the hope and the afflictions are matters of rejoicing—the first, because it orientates one towards God's glory, the second, which does the same because afflictions humble a person and throw him completely on the mercies of God, producing perseverance, character and hope (v.4). There follow two statements on *love*, to which we have added one from chapter 8.

1 How can we be certain of this hope? The answer comes in verse 5: 'because God has poured out his love into our hearts by the Holy Spirit, whom he has given us'. The words 'poured out' are usually used of the Holy Spirit (e.g. Joel 2.28). C. K. Barrett suggests Paul might have said, more clearly, 'that the Spirit had been poured out into our hearts, and that by this means God's love for us had thus become fully operative, both in making us aware of its presence, and in transforming us. Those whom he so loves God will not disappoint in the hope they set upon him.'

2 The next three verses (6–8) are a powerful argument to prove that God loves us, sinful as we are, culminating in the classic statement about God's love: 'God demonstrates his own love for us in this: While we were still sinners, Christ died for us' (v.8). Christ's death came 'at just the right time' (see Wednesday, and compare Gal. 4.4). God always comes in on cue. And what Paul says here about it is not intended to be a rationale of the crucifixion but to drive home the fact that Jesus went to such lengths to reveal God's love for us. It is such a demonstration of love that takes a Christian more than a lifetime to assimilate.

3 A further statement on our inseparability from the love of
   God (8.35–9) brings to a close this section on salvation
   (chapters 5 to 8), one of the most memorable passages in all
   Paul's writings. First he lists the adversities which may be
   encountered by those who commit their life to Christ (v.35).
   Paul knew all of these, except the last which seems to be a
   prophetic utterance concerning the way he was to meet his
   death under Nero in the 60s AD. The love of Christ enables us
   to overcome these.

   Then he lists the spiritual powers and afflictions, so dominant in the life of first-century Hellenistic man. God's gospel
   of love, shown forth in Christ, must have come as a mighty
   deliverance from all those fears and fantasies and fates. But
   it also has a message for today when evil powers are again
   being invoked by Satanic groups and devilish siren voices are
   after the hearts and minds of young people.

   In these situations, Paul's assurance comes as a shaft of
   light, piercing the gloom. *Nothing*, nothing in all creation,
   nothing in this life or the next, *nothing* can 'separate us from
   the love of God that is in Christ Jesus our Lord' (v.39). And
   that is a message of hope so many need to hear today. It is a
   message entrusted to us to deliver, not only by what we say,
   not only by what we do, but also by what we are.

Reflect on   Psalm 139.7–10

Prayer
   You have so filled the universe in every direction, Jesus, that
   henceforth it is blessedly impossible for us to escape you.
   'Where can I go to flee from your face?' Now I know for
   certain: neither life, whose advance increases your hold on me;
   nor death, which throws me into your hands; nor the good or
   evil spiritual powers which are your living instruments; nor the
   energies of matter into which you have plunged; . . . nor the
   unfathomable abysses of space which are the measure of your
   greatness, neither death, nor life, nor angels, nor principalities,
   nor things present, nor things to come, nor powers, nor height,
   nor depth, nor any creature—none of these things will be able
   to separate me from your substantial love, because they are all
   only the veil, the 'species', under which you take hold of me in
   order that I may take hold of you.
   Teilhard de Chardin

God is love
1 JOHN 4.7–21

The theme of love is a golden thread which runs right through this epistle and here we come to a passage of pure gold. The writer sees God's love as God himself, going forth from himself in redeeming action. His love will make demands on us, because it is ineffective unless we are willing to be transformed by it. The passage falls into three sections:

1 *Love one another* (vv.7–12). Our love for our brother is really a gift from God and is therefore inseparable from God's love. The two are intertwined, 'love comes from God', 'everyone who loves has been born of God and knows God', 'God is love' (vv.7,8).

The word for 'love' is again this *agapē* (see Thursday) which Bishop Stephen Neill once described as 'the steady direction of the will towards another's lasting good'. It involves acceptance of the other, not approval; the emotional element is omitted in the definition, for it centres on the will, which will persist in persevering, despite failures.

This definition fits very well the nature of God's love for us—see verses 9 and 10, where we have classic definitions of God's love. He took no account of our worthiness before he loved us (that was a mercy!); he did not ponder whether he approved or disapproved of us (another mercy!). His steadfast will was set for our lasting good: 'he loved us and sent his Son as an atoning sacrifice for our sins'. This must be the basis of our love for one another (v.11), outgoing, persevering, a matter of the will. This will open the way for the divine life to live in us (v.12).

2 *Abiding in love* (vv.13–16). The mutual abiding (v.13), God in us and we in God, is a gift of the Spirit and a token of the Spirit's presence (see yesterday, section 1). For a Christian the abiding is a fact, but it needs cultivating into consciousness. We do this by acknowledging and testifying that Jesus is ours and the world's Saviour (v.14); otherwise a dormant Christian means dormant love. As in marriage, to keep our love at full strength it has to be demonstrated. A Christian demonstrates his love by actively witnessing to his Saviour's love. The act of witness is a demonstration that 'God lives in him and he in God' (v.15). Of course the witness does not have to be vocal: sometimes a silent witness can be as effective. The purpose

should be to show others just how utterly we 'rely on the love God has for us'. In other words we rely on God who is love (v.16).

3 *The perfecting of love* (vv.17–21). The way 'love is made complete among us' (v.17) is through the 'mutual abiding' spoken of in the previous verse. And if 'in this world we are like him' (v.17) we must expect similar treatment. The world did not welcome Christ; it will not welcome his followers.

In the following verse John tackles the subject of fear, and by way of emphasis mentions it three times (and nowhere else in his epistle). Fear is repudiated because it is incompatible with love which drives it out. If we have fears, we are 'not made perfect in love' (v.18). This is a subject for self-examination, for many of us allow fears to linger in our mind or on our heart—fear of disease, of dying, of losing a loved one, or a hundred and one silly foibles. John would have us allow the love of God to drive them all out. This is certainly a necessary step for our spiritual maturity. And God's love is always first on the scene inspiring ours (v.19).

The last two verses (20 and 21) return us to the subject of love for our brother which John insists on as a proof of our love for God. If a person does not love his brother whom he has seen, it is pure fantasy to declare his love for the unseen God. But no one pretends it is easy. How shall we learn to love our brothers and sisters, especially the awkward ones— a colleague at work, a difficult member of the family, an impossible employer or employee? We could pray for them each day, remembering that Christ died for them also.

Reflect on
Where there is no love, pour love in, and you will draw out love.
St John of the Cross

Prayer
Love divine, all loves excelling,
Joy of heaven, to earth come down,
Fix in us thy humble dwelling,
All thy faithful mercies crown.
Charles Wesley

GROUP QUESTIONS

The adventure of loving

1 How can we be more deeply sensitive to the grace of God and allow for the unexpected in the planning of our own lives and the life of our church? (Monday)

2 What are the kinds of experience in loving and forgiving that teach us more about God, and bring us nearer to the heart of God? (Tuesday)

3 Have we learned the generosity of receiving? Have we allowed Jesus to 'wash' us deeply and inwardly? (Wednesday)

4 Discuss the characteristics of love (*agapē*) as detailed in the middle section of Paul's hymn to love, 1 Cor. 13.4–7. (Thursday)

5 To what extent do we really believe our inseparability from God's love, which shields and enfolds us in every situation? (Friday)

6 What are our fears? Are we allowing God's love to overcome them? (Saturday)

7 Have you any good suggestions for loving our awkward neighbour. (Saturday)

WEEK FIVE

Read   Psalm 4

Reflect on

If withdrawal into silence is focus or concentrate of experience, then it is a necessary and natural need, not an artificially imposed religious duty. Silence is the environment of creativity, the essential condition for letting-be, the birthplace of love. One does not usually compose poetry on Paddington station in the rush hour, although such experience may well provide the initial inspiration for a poem. Sleep and waking, incubation and birth, winter and summer, rest and action, habitual awareness of Being and acts of penitence and praise: this is the natural order of things. Those who run from silence are the real escapists for they dare not confront reality.

It is common experience to ordinary Christians in retreat, or after a prolonged period of silent prayer, for things, beings, creation, to take on a new and more vivid appearance. The cultivation of a deep interior silence issues in a new look towards everything, the presence and manifestation of Being in the beings is constant, but here is a positive response to that constancy. Under such conditions Julian contemplated her hazel nut; to George Fox things had 'another smell than before'; St Francis called wind and water brother and sister, not out of sentiment, but as a theological expression of contemplation; to John Scotus Erigena the world became 'a theophany'. In Buber's terminology they had all moved into an I–Thou relationship. In Macquarrie's, human being became united with other beings and glimpsed Being. In all cases it is prayer, emphatic and contemplative.

Martin Thornton, *Prayer: A New Encounter*, pp.167f.

Prayer

O Lord God, who art a hearer not of the voice but of the heart: make us grateful for the grace of prayer; whereby all impediments are removed, so that nothing can separate us from thy goodness, for time and for eternity.   Amen.

Dame Gertrude More (1606–33, Abbess, great-great-granddaughter of St Thomas More)

The Adventure of Spreading the Good News

The year of the Lord's favour
ISAIAH 61

It is hard for us to dissociate these words from Jesus' first sermon in the Nazareth synagogue and we shall come to that in due course. But what did these words imply for Isaiah (he was in fact the third Isaiah) and his contemporaries?

Isaiah prophesied at the time when the Jews had returned from exile in Babylon back to Jerusalem. It was in 538 BC that Cyrus, King of Persia, allowed them to return home and issued his edict about rebuilding the temple. Isaiah (Trito-Isaiah as the scholars call him) in all probability prophesied about 530 BC.

Amidst the general euphoria of the home-coming, Isaiah's message is one of salvation. The temple is to be rebuilt and a new age of Israelite history is dawning. God's glory will shine over his people (60.1f.) and other nations will come to this light (60.3).

In his whole message (chapters 56–66), our present passage is one of the very few that tell us anything about the prophet himself. The prophet has a positive awareness of God's strong hand upon him. His Sovereign Lord has sent and equipped him to proclaim this message of salvation (v.1). This age of salvation will bring change to the lot of those who suffer. The poor will hear the good news, the broken-hearted will receive inner healing; the captives will experience freedom again, the blind will receive their sight back (v.1), the mourners will find comfort (v.2).

The proclamation of the year of the Lord's favour heralds a new era and the day of vengeance foretold in the parallel originally meant 'the restoration of wholeness' (v.2). The following verse (3) shows how the prophet had meditated on this message of wholeness for God's people, who will receive 'a crown of beauty', 'the oil of gladness', 'a garment of praise'. They will be called 'oaks of righteousness, a planting of the Lord for the display of his splendour'.

The prophet sees the nation as having a ministry and mission to other nations. Once the temple and city is rebuilt (v.4), others will come and tend the flocks and be their vinedressers (v.5), and they will have a ministry to these aliens (v.6) while profiting from their service. In fact so dramatic will be the change in Israel's fortunes that she will be known by all as the nation which God has blessed (vv.7–9). Verse 11 should follow here.

Verse 10 is a hymn of praise sung by the community God has so blessed, a hymn of praise accepting the message of salvation, somewhat reminiscent of Mary's hymn of praise after receiving Gabriel's message of salvation for the whole human race in which she would play her part.

In Luke 4.16ff. Jesus finds that his work can be described in the very same words which Isaiah used five and a half centuries earlier. Here was an expression of the Kingdom conditions which Jesus then proclaimed as present fact: 'Today this Scripture is fulfilled in your hearing' (Luke 4.21). The proclaiming of the good news, the healings and exorcisms, all are signs that Jesus is the anointed one—that is, the Christ.

Apart from anything else, it shows Isaiah to have been within the prophetic tradition and to have played no small part in forging Israel's historical consciousness. They were a missionary nation, charged with being a light to the Gentiles. Tomorrow we shall read more about that light.

Reflect on
'Today this scripture is fulfilled in your hearing' (Luke 4.21).

Prayer
O Jesus Christ, who art the same yesterday, today and forever: Pour thy Spirit upon the Church that it may preach thee anew to each succeeding generation. Grant that it may interpret the eternal gospel in terms relevant to the life of each new age, and as the fulfilment of the highest hopes and the deepest needs of every nation; so that at all times and in all places men may see in thee their Lord and Saviour.   Amen.
George Appleton

The light in the Temple
LUKE 2.22–52

These two events are separated by twelve years. Both occurred in the Temple and Jesus is the key figure in both, passive in the first, active in the second. On each occasion the good news is being proclaimed.

The first story contains three motifs, Mary's purification, the presentation of the first-born child and the offering of the child to God for his service, as Samuel was offered to God by his parents. The Church commemorates this event on February 2nd, which is sometimes called Candlemass because candles are lighted and held at the Eucharist during the recitation of this passage.

There are several points to notice in the story:

1 The Holy Spirit is mentioned three times in connection with this holy man, Simeon: 'the Holy Spirit was upon him' (v.25), he was told by the Holy Spirit 'he would not die before he had seen the Lord's Christ' (v.26), and he was 'moved by the Spirit' to go into the temple courts just at the right moment (v.27). Holiness is a nearness to God and it is the Holy Spirit who draws a person within the sphere of the grace of our Lord Jesus Christ and fills the heart with the love of God. Simeon knew what it was to receive this blessing of the Holy Spirit. Holiness is the most effective communicator of the good news.

2 He was moved to come in at the exact time, the right time (once again), God's time (v.27). Being the right time, he was led to meet the Lord's Christ, his heart's desire. A sensitivity to the Holy Spirit's leading improves a person's timing, in what he says or refrains from saying, in what he does or refrains from doing.

3 Simeon's act of praise and thanks to God takes the form of a poetic prayer which falls into three couplets (vv.29–32). It has been a much loved canticle in public worship, or prayer in private devotion, from the earliest times.

4 Simeon's prophecy faces the negative side of Jesus' ministry, taking up the thought of the chief corner-stone also being a rock that causes men to stumble (compare Isa. 8.14 with Isa. 28.16) and of the sign that will be spoken against (v.34). The direct and poignant word to his mother (v.35) must have lain on her heart until it was fulfilled in her vigil by the cross (see John 19.25–7).

5   The ancient Anna was also guided to come up at that moment. Another holy person, who fasted and prayed, spending her time in the Temple courts, Anna also prophesied about the child to the expectant crowd (vv.36–8). For their expectation see Isa. 52.8–10.

A summary verse 39 concludes the story and Luke adds that even from a child Jesus was filled with wisdom and grace (v.40).

The story of Jesus' visit to the Temple when he was twelve years old concludes our passage and indeed the birth narratives of Luke's Gospel (vv.41–52). It is the only glimpse we have of Jesus between his presentation in the Temple and the beginning of his ministry. It throws valuable light on his spiritual maturity at the age of twelve (perhaps we underestimate our own children's spiritual sensitivity at a similar age) and shows the developing relationship with his heavenly Father. It is as though the break with his earthly home is already being made in his first recorded words (v.49). The tension between the closer relationship with his Father and obedience to his parents is already there. His parents' reaction underlines this (v.50).

Luke concludes the narrative with a statement of Jesus' obedience to his parents and a comment on his mother's deepest thoughts. Mary must now have realized her son had an even bigger obedience to offer his heavenly Father (v.51).

Finally a comment on Jesus' growth. Note how rounded and holistic it was. He grew in wisdom (the mind) and stature (the body). He also grew in favour with God (spiritually) and with men (socially) (v.52). How much of the education and home nurturing of our children today offers the possibility of growth in all these four areas? If we are parents, we might do well to ponder, like Mary, on Jesus' growth in his adolescence.

Reflect on   verse 52
What about *my own* growth in these four areas?

Prayer
Holy Spirit, thank you for drawing me into the love
of the heavenly Father through Jesus his Son.
Help me to grow as he did,
into wholeness of being and maturity of personhood,
that I may be equipped for the adventure
of spreading the good news,
in his Name.   Amen.

The sending of the disciples
LUKE 9.1–6; 10.1–11

Luke invariably gives extra space in his writings to what he regards as supremely important. In Acts, for instance, he gives two whole chapters (3 and 4) to show how obedient were the disciples to Jesus' commission to them, given here, to preach *and* heal; while the Conversion of Saul is narrated three times (Acts 9, 22 and 26) and the Cornelius episode twice (Acts 10 and 11).

The sending out of the disciples on the adventure of spreading the good news was, once again, so paramount in Luke's eyes that he (alone) records the sending not only of the Twelve but also of a further group of seventy-two. This also marks a development in the gospel narrative: hitherto Jesus' ministry has been largely among the people; from now on Jesus prepares for the 'tomorrow' of the Church and the emphasis increasingly falls on his relationship with, and his training of, the disciples. This, together with the fact that Jesus is training them for missionary adventure, lies at the heart of Luke's present desire to impress his readers with the importance of what he is saying.

The Twelve experience the power and authority Jesus gives them in anticipation of the outpouring of the Spirit (Acts 2) for their wider mission (v.1). The importance of the narrative lies in the instructions the disciples receive for their mission, instructions which all the Evangelists obviously considered as of lasting value for the Church. (The parallel passages are in Mark 6.7–13 and Matthew 10.1–14.) It will be helpful if we look at the instructions in both these chapters as a whole. What are the salient points?

1 The disciples are commanded to preach the kingdom of God (9.2; 10.9). In the latter verse they are told to proclaim the immanence of the Kingdom, possibly just to the sick who have been healed, because their healing is a sign of the Kingdom breaking into the present. However, in view of the instructions to the Twelve, it is obviously also a general instruction, to proclaim the Kingdom to everyone.

This injunction follows Jesus' own practice; he had come to set the world to rights and he did this by proclaiming the Kingdom, his Father's reign. In effect he is saying: 'My Father wills to reign again in all his creation: that means in you, who are called to a new wholeness and holiness; in the Church, which must become a true vehicle for the mission, God's holy people; in society, whose structures must be cleansed and bring my people the blessing of peace; in all creation which will come again to adore the Father Creator.' This was the good news of Jesus which he instructed his disciples to deliver.

2   The disciples are instructed to heal the sick (9.2; 10.9). In each case this is connected with the preaching and the two are to be seen as a parallel activity. Again it is consonant with Jesus' own practice. He spent an enormous time during his ministry in healing the sick. This should be where a large portion of the Church's ministry lies too.

We must praise God for the renewal of this ministry in the churches today, as the Anglican bishops did in the Lambeth Conference Resolution 8 in 1978. We must also praise God for Pope John Paul II's leadership in this regard. He has been called 'a healing Pope' (see Frank Lake's book *With Respect*), and during his visit to Britain the Pope held a service of healing in Southwark (R.C.) Cathedral, administering the sacrament of anointing. In this ministry lies an awareness of, and obedience to, Jesus' own ministry and his instructions to the disciples (all disciples) for their mission. 'The disciples' task was to preach *and* to heal and there is no conflict between the two' (I. Howard Marshall). They must go together.

3   The disciples are to travel light (9.3; 10.4). Other missionaries at that time made a profit from their preaching: not so the disciples of Christ. A detachment from the things of this world increases the disciple's attachment to God. 'Enough is enough.'

4   When they enter a house they are to stay there, not moving round from house to house (from parish to parish?) (9.4; 10.7). This means they must exercise a degree of contentment, mingled with genuine gratitude, such as will commend their message.

5   Finally, if they receive a hostile reception, they are to use the Jewish symbolic act as a sign of lack of fellowship between God and those who don't wish to know him (9.5; 10.10–12).

Luke will again take up the great theme of evangelism and the Church's missionary task in Acts, as the adventure of spreading the good news unfolds.

Reflect on

The golden rule is to start small. Although Jesus spent some time with the crowds, and at least on one occasion sent out seventy disciples on a specific mission, it is clear that he spent most of his ministry on this earth with the small band of twelve. And of those twelve, he concentrated especially on three, James, Peter and John. Those three were with him in the sickroom of Jairus' daughter, on the Mount of Transfiguration, and in the Garden of Gethsemane. No doubt Jesus risked the jealousy of the other nine by giving certain privileges to those three; no doubt he caused envious questions to be asked by other followers when he spent so much time with the twelve. But it is impossible to disciple more than a small group at any given time if those disciples are to grow into true spiritual maturity. On those twelve depended the whole future of the Christian church. One failed completely and all the others were disappointments from time to time. But as Jesus persisted with them, loving them to the end, he was laying a firm foundation for the whole church of God.

Any wise leader will likewise concentrate his time with a small group of committed Christians, twelve probably being the maximum number for effective discipling. In fact, the fewer the better.

David Watson, *Discipleship*, p.77

Prayer

Lord Jesus, who chose twelve disciples and sent them forth to preach the gospel and to heal the sick: Forgive the faithless disobedience of thy children, and help us to restore the healing ministry to thy Church. Grant that thy whole Church as thy body may be inspired to teach and to heal; that again signs may follow upon faith in thee, and the world may know that thou art our mighty Saviour; to whom be all praise and glory, now and for evermore. Amen.

Guild of Health

The good news of Easter
MATTHEW 28.1–10, 16–20

The cross and resurrection, and it is hard to separate the two in our thought and devotion, was the mighty event of the New Testament which launched the good news of Jesus Christ upon the world. It also began the greatest adventure to which man has ever been summoned: the spreading of that good news.

Think for a moment of the cost of this adventure to so many men and women down the ages: the apostles themselves, only one of whom avoided a martyr's death; those who suffered in the Roman persecution of the first three centuries; those who have suffered for the particular brand of Christianity they have professed, usually at the hands of their fellow Christians; those who have suffered and continue to suffer in our day from oppression by a political power. How Christians need the Holy Spirit of adventure in their task of mission!

The first two who received, and who were charged with spreading, the good news were women, a sobering thought for a consistently male-dominated Church. (A look at the Yin and Yang influences in Chinese philosophy may offer a necessary corrective to the imbalances we have experienced for too long in the West. For those interested in the shifting trends of our civilization, *The Turning Point* by Fritjof Capra (Wildwood House, London) will be found informative and fascinating.) The two Marys had been present at the cross, at his burial and now were receiving the reward of love. William Barclay has remarked on three imperatives given to the women in this resurrection narrative:

1 They were urged not to fear but *to believe* (vv.5 and 6). The angel's message is almost a credal statement, reminding them of just what Jesus had said: 'Jesus, who was crucified . . . has risen'. The empty tomb is then offered as proof.

   Many still have a 'fear' or doubt about this central event of our faith. The only way to dispel it is to take Christ at his word. 'I believe and trust in Him.' Our intuition, also, needs to be used alongside our intellect, to produce a balanced judgement.

2 They are urged *to share* the good news (v.7). 'Go quickly and tell' is the word that sets anyone who is possessed with the truth of Christ straight off on the great adventure of sharing and spreading that good news. Never, never can we selfishly

keep it to ourselves. It is for my brother and sister, for my neighbour, for my colleague at work and for the whole world. 'Go quickly and tell . . .' Who will it be *today*? 'Go and tell my brothers . . .' says Jesus (v.10).

3   They are urged *to rejoice*. The first word spoken by the Risen Christ was a joyful greeting (v.9), *chairete* in the Greek. The literal meaning is 'rejoice'. The person who has met the risen Christ is a transformed being, with an infectious radiance and serenity. Like St Paul, who met him on the Damascus road he may be 'sorrowful, yet always rejoicing; poor, yet making many rich, having nothing and yet possessing everything' (2 Cor. 6.10—see Friday in Week 2).

We come now to the final words of Matthew's Gospel and Jesus' commission to his disciples (vv.16–20). To all, including some who are doubtful (v.17), he first gives an assurance of his authority (v.18), an authority which rests on his life, death and resurrection and therefore is backed by the power that raised him from the dead. Because the resurrection is a cosmic event similar to the creation (it is sometimes called the second creation) it is also universal, for all peoples and for all time. It is not merely a peg on which to hang the Christian faith. The resurrection has given Jesus authority as the cosmic Christ.

Secondly, Jesus gives the disciples a commission (vv.19f.), 'to make disciples of all nations'. The universal Lord claims all peoples for his Father's Kingdom. The Church's mission is therefore to the world. The Church is apostolic and every member is *sent* into the world to engage in the adventure of spreading the good news.

Thirdly, he does not leave us alone to do this; he gives a promise that he will be with us always, 'to the very end of the age' (v.20). The greatest task will need the greatest Presence.

Reflect on

Christ today is reigning in heaven. One day, at the name of Jesus every knee shall bow and every tongue shall confess that Jesus Christ is Lord. Until that glorious and awesome day, he has both commissioned us with the task of proclaiming him to the world as Lord and Saviour, and equipped us with all that we need to accomplish that task. 'This Jesus God raised up, and of that we all are witnesses. Being therefore exalted at the right hand of God, and having received from the Father the promise of the Holy Spirit, he has poured out this which you see and hear.' So Peter was able to preach on the day of Pentecost. It is this same Spirit of the living God that needs to fall afresh on us today, if our belief in evangelism is to bear fruit. God has not withdrawn his gift or his promise. He waits for us, his children, to come to him with all our obvious need; and he will then give the Holy Spirit to those who ask him.

David Watson, *I Believe in Evangelism*, p.186

Prayer

Father, you have committed to men
    the good news of your saving love
and set us as ambassadors for Christ
    in your world:
help us together to bear witness
    to the message of reconciliation,
that in the life of your Church
    men may become new creatures
    in Jesus Christ our Lord.

Contemporary Parish Prayers, no.465

The power from on high
ACTS 1.6–9; 2.1–11

Yesterday we read the final words of Matthew's Gospel, in which Jesus gave the disciples a commission before his ascension. Luke ends his Gospel at the same place and records the ascension and the disciples return to Jerusalem 'with great joy' in their hearts (Luke 24.50–3).

Now Luke takes up the story in his second volume, beginning at the same place, with the meeting on the mount of the ascension (Acts 1.6–9). The question of the disciples may seem to be materialistic (v.6), but they had been schooled well enough in the theology of the Kingdom and Jesus' reply about 'the times and dates' (v.7) may refer to the stages of spiritual development that are necessary for everyone to undergo before an acceptance of the Kingdom conditions is possible. I once heard Metropolitan Anthony warn a conference of priests not to pray for a vision of the living Christ for which they would be totally unprepared and unready.

The disciples had in fact not yet received the Holy Spirit, who would bring them the presence of Christ, but this is promised in the very next verse (8) as the power (from on high). This power will be given for one essential purpose: to equip the disciples to bear witness to the risen Christ throughout the world (as in Matthew's version, yesterday). Note the ever enlarging concentric circles mapped out for the Christian witness: Jerusalem, Judea, Samaria, to the ends of the earth. Also worthy of note is the fact that to be a witness, you have to have first-hand experience: hearsay is no good, as we soon find out if we are unfortunate enough to be in the witness box in a court of law. That is the reason for the power from on high: to equip them, and now us, to be witnesses to the risen Christ.

At the beginning of Chapter 2, Luke records the outpouring of this power from on high upon the disciples. The 'all' in verse 1 probably includes Mary the mother of Jesus, the other women and various others, though not all scholars agree with this; while 'together' is a semi-liturgical word that in Acts means something like 'gathered together in church or as a body'.

Luke is a good historian and must have questioned the disciples keenly about this event. From their witness he decides to describe the coming of the Holy Spirit in terms of 'violent wind' (v.2), as the breath of God was experienced in Old Testament times; and also as tongues of fire (v.3) resting on each of them, as the divine presence or Shekinah rested on the pious Jew studying the Law. The experience is reminiscent of that of Elijah (see Tuesday in Week 3).

The basic fact is that all were filled with the Spirit (v.4), and Luke, who dates this experience on the feast of Pentecost, originally a harvest festival but also associated with the giving of the Torah, one of the great days of the year for a Jew, is saying: 'Here, fifty days after the first Easter Day, occurred an event on this feast of Pentecost that will be of such great import to the Christian Church that many will even look at it as its beginning.' Pentecost is the festival indeed of the Holy Spirit: it is also the festival of the Church.

The effect of the outpouring is of very great interest. The gift of tongues (*glossolalia*) was viewed by Paul as ecstatic utterance, unintelligible to the hearer and therefore needing an interpreter. Luke understood it as the gift of foreign languages. The two ideas are not incompatible, because as those who have this experience know, certain foreign words frequently drop off the tongue when the gift is given as well as sounds that (to an outsider) are incomprehensible. Whatever may be said of the experience, it is a form of release to the individual, giving a new freedom in prayer, and, most important for our purpose here, giving a new stimulus and energy for witnessing to the risen Christ. It was this gift that enabled the Christian gospel to spread like a forest fire in the early days of the Church. In many parts of the world, such a blessing is being repeated in the churches today.

Reflect on

Almost every chapter in Acts records some manifestation of the Spirit: tongues, healings, prophecies, visions, judgements, exorcisms, miracles—all of which were powerful ways of helping people to come to a living faith in a living God.

J. B. Phillips, in his preface to his paraphrase of the Acts of the Apostles, put it like this:

These men did not make 'acts of faith', they believed; they did not 'say their prayers', they really prayed. They did not hold conferences on psychosomatic medicine, they simply healed the sick . . . No one can read this book without being convinced that there is Someone here at work besides mere human beings. Perhaps because of their very simplicity, perhaps because of their readiness to believe, to obey, to give, to suffer, and if need be to die, the Spirit of God found what he must always be seeking—a fellowship of men and

women so united in love and faith, that he can work in them
and through them with the minimum of let or hindrance.
Indeed it was precisely because of such a free and powerful
demonstration of the Spirit of God that 'more than ever
believers were added to the Lord, multitudes both of men and
women'.
David Watson, *I Believe in Evangelism*, pp.52f.

Prayer

Almighty God,
who on the day of Pentecost
sent your Holy Spirit to the disciples
with the wind from heaven and in tongues of flame,
filling them with joy
   and boldness to preach the Gospel:
send us out in the power of the same Spirit
to witness to your truth
and to draw all men to the fire of your love;
through Jesus Christ our Lord.   Amen.
2nd Collect for Pentecost (ASB)

St Paul's adventures and sufferings in spreading the good news
2 CORINTHIANS 11.21—12.10

Our reading today falls into three sections: concerning the external hazards in the adventure (11.21–33); an out-of-the-body experience (12.1–6); and internal suffering that threatened Paul and his work for the Lord (12.7–10).

1 Paul turns first to his personal credentials which had come under criticism from the Jewish party. He shows that his qualifications are equal to anyone's (v.22). He then moves on to his qualifications as a Christian. His record of service as a Christian apostle and evangelist (i.e. a spreader of the good news) is really formidable (vv.23–7). We must thank his critics for provoking such an outburst so that his experiences were committed to writing. (Critics have their uses!) In this passage we come face to face with what can befall the Christian who takes his Lord's command seriously: Go and tell. A person who feels called to the Christian adventure should ponder on these verses.

   Paul, as an apostle, adds that every day he feels the pressure of responsibility (v.28), unerringly putting his finger on the real stress that affects those who hold office in the Church—or in any 'organization'. 'The pressure of concern' is something that is now quantifiable by medical science, but cannot be assisted in the long term by medication. Only a constant distancing of oneself in the Lord, for example through a daily dose of contemplative prayer, can bear the name of a remedy and tackle the symptoms in depth. A regular reorganizing of our routine to this end is a useful beginning in alleviating any *needless* stress.

   The final verses of the chapter (30–3) are a humble assertion of his weakness, giving an example of an occasion when he did take the easy way out. But how God used it and what things were accomplished because his life was prolonged!

2 Paul then proceeds to tell of an out-of-the-body experience (12.1–6) which, in view of the introduction to it (v.1), was in all probability autobiographical. He obviously accepts that in this life the self may be separated from the physical body. There are many instances of such occurrences, especially as death comes nearer (see *To Die is Gain* by J. C. Hampe).

   Parallels to Paul's experience can in fact be cited from

many fields: from apocalyptic, which concerns God's future breaking into this world (for example, in the apocryphal book of Enoch—1 Enoch 39.3f.); from mystical speculation, not unknown among the Rabbis; from ecstasy, familiar in Hellenistic mysticism; and of course from the experience of spiritual rapture in the higher states of prayer. Despite this experience, he does not wish to flaunt it, but rather would dwell on his weaknesses (vv.5 and 6). They are however experiences that should be greatly treasured, for which one should thank and praise God the giver.

3 Finally, Paul tells us of his thorn in the flesh (vv.7–10). Very many suggestions have been made over the centuries about what this 'dis-ease' might have been. The short answer is that we don't know. The disease is as likely to have been spiritual as physical or mental, perhaps a combination of all three which attacked his whole personality. Three times he pleaded with the Lord for its removal, but the answer came, 'My grace is sufficient for you, for my power is made perfect in weakness' (v.9). What a sublime answer and what an encouragement to generations of Christians in their adventure for Christ! For this we have to thank Paul's thorn in the flesh. And what a lesson Paul learned too: 'When I am weak, then am I strong' (v.10). When our strivings cease, the Lord, who was crucified, can come in and do *his* work, something Paul learned from the martyrdom of Stephen as well as from his own experience.

Reflect on
Never look down to test the ground before taking your next step: only he who keeps his eye fixed on the far horizons will find his right road.

Never measure the height of a mountain, until you have reached the top. Then you will see how low it was.
Dag Hammarskjöld in *Markings*

Prayer
Heavenly Father,
give use grace in all our sufferings for the truth
to follow the example of your first martyr Saint Stephen:
that we also may look to him who was crucified
and pray for those who persecute us;
through Jesus Christ our Lord.   Amen.
Collect for St Stephen's Day (ASB)

GROUP QUESTIONS

The Adventure of Spreading the Good News

1 What common tasks have Isaiah's ministry and the Church's ministry today? and why? (Monday)

2 How fully are we encouraging the holistic growth of our children, in family, in school and in the voluntary organizations we run for them? (see the second part of Tuesday's reading and comment). What about my own journey towards maturity?

3 Is there a balance in your church's (your own) ministry between preaching and healing? Is there a small group of 'disciples' supporting both these ministries in your locality? (Wednesday)

4 'To believe . . . to share . . . to rejoice' (Thursday). The Easter 'sequence' is a formula to help us in spreading the good news. Are all its elements included in our own and our church's mission? And do we believe in that eternal Presence with us?

5 'A fellowship of men and women so united in love and faith, that [the Holy Spirit] can work in them and through them with the minimum of let or hindrance' (Friday). Have we the experience of being part of such a fellowship?

6 What part has suffering played in your life and how has it been turned to positive good? Have you any experiences like Paul's which you can share with the group? (Saturday)

WEEK SIX

Christ's Own 'Adventure'

Cry Hosanna
MATTHEW 21.1–17

During this last week, we shall be in the company of Jesus while he goes through the final 'adventure' of his earthly life. I don't think it is blasphemous to speak of it as an adventure, because the word speaks of an *arrival at* a certain point, a *coming to* a situation, a *finding* that something has to be met, endured, for a greater purpose. In these ways Jesus must have conceived his approaching death on the cross and all that went with it—the *coming into* Jerusalem, his final teaching of the disciples, especially on the last night, and his *arrival at* Calvary.

I hope our experiences together with one another and especially with *him* in the midst, have led to the desire to be with him as he essays this final adventure that all of us must face, one way or another. We shall watch with him, always in command of the circumstances that surround the adventure and supremely in command of himself; always in intimate fellowship with his heavenly Father, the key to the whole drama; and always unfailingly loving both to his own and to those whom he longed to transform into his own, to whom he invariably showed patience and courtesy.

Today's reading records the events of the first Palm Sunday, Christ's triumphal entry into Jerusalem and the cleansing of the Temple. Note the context of these events: they come between healings of the blind (and lame), one of the express means Jesus used to proclaim the Kingdom of God and fulfil his mission (see Monday of last week).

The other synoptic writers (cf. Mark 10.46ff. and Luke 18.35ff.) record the first episode of healing the blind, as Matthew does at the close of the previous chapter (20.29–34), though he has two blind men. Matthew has a series of twos which may be explained by the fact that in all probability he was in possession of more stories of healing by Jesus than space permitted him to record.

Matthew also inserts one of his explicit summary verses to record the healing of blind and lame (21.14), but very pointedly after the cleansing of the Temple to show that once God's Temple is cleansed of all that pollutes it and of all the luggage that blocks the entry of those in need, then the true work of the Kingdom can go forward unhindered. The crowds will again cry 'Hosanna' (i.e. save/heal, 21.9) and praise God for his coming in power. Matthew obviously intended us to learn much from the event because of what led up to today's 'adventure' and of what followed.

The triumphal entry itself (vv.1–11) is self-explanatory. Notice Matthew keeps on with his doublets: two disciples are sent to find the donkey and her colt (v.2), as prophesied in Zechariah 9.9, the source of the quotation (v.5). The prophet however was only speaking in parallel lines, the method of Hebrew poetry, of the same animal. Be that as it may, Jesus seems to have used the animal(s) to make a point: he was indeed the Messiah but came not as a military leader; rather did he come humbly, as the suffering servant, to offer his life a ransom for many. The crowds were therefore right to acclaim him as Son of David (v.9); he would however answer their cries of 'Hosanna' in a different way from what they expected, in a way that Isaiah prophesied of the Servant (see Isa. 53, especially v.5).

The cleansing of the Temple (vv.12–17; cf. Mark 11.11ff., Luke 19.45ff. and John 2.13–22) follows at once in Matthew and Luke, the day after in Mark, while in John it is placed at the beginning of the Gospel as a symbol of the cleansing Jesus brought to the religion of his day. Here we see an explosion of Jesus' anger at the desecration of his Father's house. We must not gloss over this anger. The anger within us can be used as a force for good when directed in the cause of right. Here Jesus directs his anger against those who exploit their fellow men, especially in the cause of religion. He could never bear to see simple people exploited in any way; he always identified himself with the poor and the outcast. That they were prevented from worshipping in the house of God was just too much to stomach. He drives the offenders out of the Temple on the authority of Isaiah (56.7) and Jeremiah (7.11).

The eventful day ends with healing, as was said earlier. In Jesus anger and love are the different sides of the same coin. He does not drive away those in need: they remain in the Temple and have their needs fulfilled. As William Barclay commented: 'The destructive force of anger must always go hand in hand with the healing power of love.' The prayer of the crowd's Hosanna became a psalm of praise (vv.15, 16), and no wonder.

Reflect on

Is my house a house of prayer? Or do I need to do something before it can become so? And what about the church where I worship? Is prayer and praise a priority?

Prayer

Lord, on this Palm Sunday you were given a hero's welcome as one who was going the way of the crowd; but you had chosen the way of the cross, and the applause was short-lived.

Keep bright and clear before us the vision of our calling, that we may never be diverted from the way you have chosen for us, but may follow in the steps of you, our crucified and risen Lord, to whom be all glory, laud and honour, this day and for evermore.   Amen.

Basil Naylor

The cost of discipleship
MATTHEW 16.13–28

In the synoptic Gospels (see Mark 8.27–30; Luke 9.18–21), Peter's confession of faith at Caesarea Philippi marks a significant point of development in the training of the disciples. From now on Jesus prepares them for the cross.

'*Jesus . . . asked*' (v.13). The imperfect tense is used with the implication Jesus kept on asking them. He wanted to hear it from them. The answers begin to come—John the Baptist, Elijah, Jeremiah, one of the prophets (v.14). He accepted the title of prophet, but was still conscious of a unique calling, so he pressed them for an answer: 'But you . . .' (v.15).

'*Simon Peter answered . . .*' (v.16). His great confession of faith comes loud and clear, 'You are the Christ', the Messiah, the Lord's Anointed. Christ comes from a word meaning to rub, especially of oil. Just as kings and priests of old were anointed with oil (our Sovereign is still anointed during the coronation ceremony), so Jesus is God's very special, anointed Son, the Christ. He is therefore also 'the Son of the living God'; his nature and his relationship with the Father are unique.

'*Jesus replied . . .*' (vv.17–19). These verses appear only in Matthew's Gospel, but it is not necessary to doubt their authenticity. Jesus praises Peter for his basic, if partial, understanding, and perhaps too for his courage in speaking out before them all. God, Jesus says, has given him the insight to make this confession of faith. His name is to be the Rock (Petros in Greek, Cephas in Aramaic) and on this Rock, who is Peter, the first to confess Jesus as Christ, Jesus can build his Church. In a sense the Church began right there. Peter did in fact exercise fruitful leadership in the first critical days of the Church; this is recorded in Acts. For this we must rejoice and pray that this saying of Jesus shall never be used to sunder the Church which Christ is building. The power of the keys must be used so that, even in wrath, mercy is remembered (see Habakkuk 3.2). In the meantime, the disciples' understanding of the Christ is only partial; they do not comprehend the element of suffering in the Messianic vocation and so they must refrain from telling people that Jesus is the Christ. (v.20).

'*Jesus began to explain . . .*' (vv.21–3). 'From that time' the teaching and training of the disciples deepens. The second part of the gospel story, which will end in the cross and resurrection, now begins to unfold. 'He must . . . suffer' is a statement of the divine will and purpose. Mark attaches such importance to Jesus' words that he records them three times (Mark 8.31, 9.31 and 10.33). The words form the theme of Jesus' teaching from now on. He must meet suffering and death. Every disciple too must face these facts, for Jesus and for himself, if he is to grow in maturity. The depth of a person's spiritual maturity will often depend on whether suffering and death have been faced and *gone through* in Christ. The maturity of a marriage will also depend on whether the partners have faced it together. Have I? Have we? Peter still had to face this and at that moment refused to do so. He was proving a stumbling block to Christ's progress as well as to his own maturity in discipleship. He was therefore accorded a stunning rebuke. It is the things of God, not of men, which are paramount for a disciple (v.23).

'*Jesus said to his disciples* . . .' (vv.24–8). First, a disciple is to deny himself. This means, in psychological terms, that we must deny our 'ego', the part of us which is trying to dominate our personality in self-destructive ways, in order to realize our true self, which is our full personality, made in the image of God and renewed in Christ.

Secondly, he is to take up his cross, that is, face a life of service and sacrifice, in which success may not be granted. This may sound morbid, but in this way lies the whole secret of adventure and the end is resurrection, the ever-new and glorious joy of life in Christ. The way of self-seeking on the contrary leads to self-destruction.

Thirdly, he must follow Christ. George Bennett used to have two words that were special to him: awareness and obedience. Following Christ demands a constant awareness of him, where he is leading, what he is saying, wherein lies his will for us. The rest is a loving obedience to his promptings (v.24).

Now comes the whole paradox of the Christian adventure: trying to follow in our own way, with built-in safeguards (v.25) or through the enjoyment of worldly success (v.26) will lead to a loss of the whole enterprise. Only obedient surrender of life, even of what and whom we hold most dear, for the sake of Christ's call to discipleship, can bring the hoped-for blessing of life, real life, eternal life. And only that kind of life is the real life, life worth living. What utter joy there is once life is surrendered, a joy which Christ shares in his Father's glory with the angels (v.27) and which will be the Kingdom experience (v.28).

Reflect on   Verses 24 to 28 of this passage.

Prayer

Almighty God,
who inspired your apostle Saint Peter
to confess Jesus as Christ and Son of the living God:
build up your Church upon this rock,
that in unity and peace
it may proclaim one truth and follow one Lord,
your Son our Saviour Jesus Christ,
who is alive and reigns with you and the Holy Spirit,
one God, now and for ever.   Amen.

Collect for St Peter's Day (ASB)

This is my Son . . . Listen to him
MATTHEW 17.1–13

It will be noted that today's reading follows immediately after
the passage we thought about yesterday. (It is also recorded in
Mark 9.2–8 and Luke 9.28–36.) In one way it can therefore be
seen as a deepening of the disciples' experience and teaching by
Jesus; it is this, and yet so much more.

Bishop Michael Ramsey has noted that the event brings all
things together—the living and the dead, the old and the new,
suffering and glory, the age to come and the present, the human
and the divine. It was this that led me to see it as a model for
healing (in *The Christian Healing Ministry*, pp.193ff.), for it does
indeed draw so many dimensions together. Let us attempt to
gather a few.

First, it is good to remember how Jesus prepared the chosen
three (v.1) for the event. The two facts they had just learned and
were absorbing into their consciousness were that Jesus was the
Christ and that the Christ must suffer. They would also be
weighing up the cost of following such a person (see 16.24–6 in
yesterday's reading). Now he has selected just three of them, the
size of an intimate family, and gives them some physical exercise
by taking them up a mountain. In doing all this, he has in fact
brought all strands of their personalities together, by seeing to
their mental, emotional and physical needs. Well, all except one,
the spiritual, to which we now turn.

Luke (9.29) tells us that Jesus was praying. He constantly was
in a state of prayer and Luke remarks on it frequently. In this
state Jesus was transfigured, shot through, with light and the glory
to come (v.2). It was a precious moment of supreme awareness
and deep insight into the resurrection life of glory. It is the
experience of the spiritual in which all things are brought
together—in Christ. In this vision of Christ in glory the future
breaks into the present, bringing together the life of the world to
come with the present.

Then Moses and Elijah appear (v.3). The Law and the Prophets,
the old and the new, the static and the moving in religious
experience, are brought together in an experience that unites the
material and spiritual world, the dead and the living. The secret
of all this 'healing' is the transfigured Christ. In *him* there is
always a new creation (2 Cor. 5.17). In *him*, life is all of a piece,
whole, eternal. Luke adds they were talking about the 'Exodus'
Jesus was to bring to fulfilment (Luke 9.31), thus linking the

mighty works of the old and new covenants, the Exodus from the slavery of Egypt with the Redemption wrought by the cross/resurrection. The event is like a magnifying glass, focusing all the rays of the sun in one point.

Peter always has something to say (v.4), and not for the first time is he interrupted by divine action (v.5; see Acts 10.44). A cloud, the traditional symbol of God's presence, envelops them (v.5) and the voice is heard: 'This is my Son . . . Listen to him'. It is the same voice as at his baptism, approving his ministry; now it confirms his teaching about the divine will that he must suffer. The reaction of the disciples is one of fear which Jesus dispels (vv.6, 7). The vision ends with them seeing Jesus only; all had been brought together in him, including the answers to their unspoken questions, the quieting of their minor rebellion against his having to suffer, the vision and assurance of glory to come. Now they understand (v.13).

The mountain experience has to be left behind (v.9). The disciples however were now better equipped to face whatever might come in life on the plain. So our own precious moments with Christ, the joyous times when his presence seems 'nearer than breathing, closer than hands and feet', are occasions that equip us better to be his servants, to carry on his work in the world in the light of the glory of the world to come, because they bring together the various strands of life's adventure in that they unite us to Christ.

Let us look out for the transfiguring moments when that glory is glimpsed and treasure them, for, as Calvin remarked, 'The world is the theatre of the divine glory'.

Reflect on

O wondrous type, O vision fair
Of glory that the Church shall share,
Which Christ upon the mountain shows,
Where brighter than the sun he glows!

The law and prophets there have place,
The chosen witnesses of grace;
The Father's voice from out the cloud
Proclaims his only Son aloud.

With shining face and bright array,
Christ deigns to manifest today
What glory shall to faith be given
When we enjoy our God in heaven.

And Christian hearts are raised on high
By that great vision's mystery,
For which in thankful strains we raise
On this glad day the voice of praise.

15th-century hymn: *Caelestis formam gloriae*

Prayer

Almighty Father,
whose Son was revealed in majesty
  before he suffered death upon the cross:
give us faith to perceive his glory,
that we may be strengthened to suffer with him
and be changed into his likeness, from glory to glory;
who is alive and reigns with you and the Holy Spirit,
one God, now and for ever.

Collect for the Transfiguration (ASB)

This is my body
MATTHEW 26.17–30

The constant mention of time in these opening verses heightens the tension as Jesus approaches the cross. It is now 'the first day of the Feast of Unleavened Bread' (v.17), and 'the Passover' was eaten on the evening of that day. The disciples are to say, 'My appointed time is near' (v.18).

Jesus himself was always conscious of his time (that is, the right time; see Friday in Week 3). He began his ministry when he felt the time was right (Mark 1.15). Paul saw that God sent his Son just at the right time (Gal. 4.4). So now, the appointed time, according to the Father's will, for the mighty work of the New Covenant, the second Exodus by the second Moses, is imminent. The disciples obey Jesus' directions and prepare the Passover (v.19), commemorating the time when the first-born sons of the Israelites were spared (Exod. 12.27). This time God was not even to spare his only-begotten Son.

There follows the confronting of Judas (vv.20–5), who unwittingly becomes an instrument for hastening on the time. Again the mention of time, the fact that the evening drew on and the darkness fell, heightens the drama. Jesus does for Judas what he does for us all in temptation, provided we are prepared to listen to the voice of conscience, the means he has of prompting us. He first confronts Judas with his sin, declaring quite openly what he is about to do and allowing him to face the enormity of his deed (v.21). Then he confronts Judas with himself (vv.23f.). If 'betrayal' is the name of the deed, traitor is the name of the doer. Treachery and murder are the ultimate in sin against our neighbour and above all against God. Judas is given a chance to see this and the awful punishment (self-inflicted) that will ensue. Above all he is given a chance to see Jesus, as the three saw him on the Mount of Transfiguration. Tragically he declines. It is the hour of darkness.

The time, the traitor, and now the Thanksgiving. Jesus celebrates the Passover meal, the Last Supper, with his disciples (vv.26–30). Notice first how he does four things as he did at the feeding of the five thousand (14.19), giving our contemporary Eucharist what is sometimes known as the 'four-action shape'. Jesus *took* bread (the Offertory or Preparation of the Bread and Wine); Jesus *gave thanks* (the Consecration or the Thanksgiving); Jesus *broke* it (the Fraction or the Breaking of the Bread); Jesus *gave* it (the Communion or the Giving of the Bread and Cup). The actions of Jesus at the Last Supper form the basis of our eucharistic rite. We could not have a more biblical base for the Church's central act of worship.

Jesus also declares the bread over which he gives thanks to be 'my body' and the cup over which he gives thanks to be 'my blood'. In this act he mysteriously (*mysterion/um* was the word for sacrament) interprets his approaching death and puts his disciples under obedience to 'do this' frequently for his recalling (see the earliest account of the Last Supper in 1 Cor. 11.23–6). For our spiritual health we need regularly to be present at his recalling (1 Cor. 11.26) and receive the tokens of his Presence, something about which we could often examine ourselves with profit (see John 6.53–8).

This spiritual food is also 'the medicine of immortality', a partaking in the heavenly banquet, the eschatological (of the last days) feast of the people of God. Jesus therefore points the disciples forward to the new and eternal celebration in the Father's kingdom (v.29), attended by all who have worked and prayed for the Father's reign to be re-established in his creation. For the time being, they anticipate the heavenly music by singing a hymn—how important it is that Christians should sing together when they meet—and then go forward to the necessary first step in the Kingdom's inauguration.

The Last Supper gave the disciples a proper perspective of the events in which they were caught up. It allowed them an insight into the meaning of the Passion, an assurance that Jesus' death would somehow benefit them and 'many' others, particularly through granting them forgiveness of sins (v.28), while it also pointed them forward to the final triumph in which they would share his joy.

Reflect on
O sacred feast,
wherein Christ is received,
the memory of his Passion is renewed,
our souls are fulfilled with grace,
and a pledge of future glory is given us.   Alleluia.
Antiphon: *O sacrum convivium*

Prayer
Almighty and heavenly Father,
we thank you that in this wonderful sacrament
you have given us the memorial
   of the passion of your Son Jesus Christ.

Grant us so to reverence
the sacred mysteries of his body and blood,
that we may know within ourselves
and show forth in our lives the fruits of his redemption;
who is alive and reigns with you and the Holy Spirit,
one God, now and for ever.
Collect, Thanksgiving for the Institution of Holy Communion (ASB)

Watch and pray
MATTHEW 26.36—46

In this reading we come to share Jesus' agony in the garden of Gethsemane. The name means oil-press and so the garden was an olive grove, with the press in a permanent position for use in the season. Probably Jesus was lent this garden on the Mount of Olives as a secluded and shaded retreat for him and his disciples while in Jerusalem.

Leaving eight of the disciples at the entrance to the garden—Judas had already left them—Jesus took the same three who had shared the Transfiguration experience (see Tuesday) to share the agony of the decision he must reach through prayer (vv.36,37). Sorrow, trouble, overwhelm, death—the very words of these verses (37 and 38) depict the depth of his agony. How he needs their companionship: 'Stay here and keep watch with me.'

There follows the greatest struggle of agonizing decision a man has ever had to face. Three times, showing its intensity, Jesus goes forward to agonize in prayer. The first time, he asks that, if there is another way forward to achieve his purpose, the Father will take it and remove the cup of suffering. Yet despite this strong petition, there is a willingness to obey, so that the Father is able to take the decision either way—'as you will' (v.39).

He returns to the disciples and finds them asleep. One hour! That's all he asked: not long. He rebukes Peter, but as we read it we know the reproach can also be levelled at us. An hour of prayer seems an 'eternity': and yet in terms of eternity how pitifully short (v.40). The injunction 'Watch and pray . . .' is therefore for us a needful encouragement to persist in prayer (1 Thess. 5.17). Surely Jesus' night vigil in agony will prove an inducement in the future to set aside times of prayer (v.41).

The second vigil of prayer was crucial for Jesus after the first. He could have gone outside the Father's will; it was wholly logical and reasonable for him to have done so. He was young to die, there was more work to do, his disciples were not fully trained, crucifixion was an ignominious as well as a painful death and would allow his enemies to triumph. It is easy to rationalize the will of God out of the way. Any fool can do it. But he would be a cowardly knave rather than a fool for Christ's sake. The way of courage rather than cowardice, of intuitive wisdom rather than analytical or rationalizing dexterity, is to remain within the will of God. This Jesus did in the second agony of prayer: 'My Father if it is not possible . . . may your will be done' (v.42). He had taught his disciples to pray that prayer: 'Father . . . your will be done' (Matt. 6.9ff.); now he prayed it himself.

If the second vigil of prayer was crucial, the third confirmed him in his decision to remain within his Father's will. He could look for no assistance from the special trio of his disciples, whom he found asleep again (v.43), and so he went forward alone, majestic in his solitude and yet now, perhaps for the first time, feeling desperately lonely. He used the same words, now more positively knowing that there was but one way forward (v.44). That way he could only travel alone.

Death is the certain event that comes to us all. It is equally certain that we must face it alone. How can we face it positively, as Jesus did? One consideration must be what is beyond. Jesus faced death 'for the joy set before him' (Heb. 12.2; Saturday in Week 2). Now he has actually passed through the grave and gate of death to his resurrection, he has shown us that that joy is reality. As Paul said, 'To die is gain' (Phil. 1.21). The future is assured; it is the present, the act of dying and leaving the ones we love behind that is the source of our fear.

Here we have the encouragement of Jesus' example; his strength was the close relationship he enjoyed with his heavenly Father. He had worked at this through his life; he knew how to be alone (many of us don't), and alone with his Father through long hours of prayer. This is the best, and the only preparation, for our last journey on this earth, which therefore need not be entirely alone.

Because of his faith and trust in his heavenly Father, Jesus was able to say, 'Rise, let us go' (v.46). He had a baptism to be baptized with and was under stress until it was completed (see Luke 12.50, Mark 10.38). Just as our baptism is the only way of sharing his death and resurrection and being made one with him, so his death and resurrection for him were the baptism he must undergo to remain at one with the Father's will.

Reflect on   Mark 10.38

Prayer
Grant, Lord,
   that we who are baptized into the death
      of your Son our Saviour Jesus Christ
   may continually put to death our evil desires
      and be buried with him;

104

that through the grave and gate of death
we may pass to our joyful resurrection;
through his merits, who died and was buried
    and rose again for us,
your Son Jesus Christ our Lord.   Amen.
Collect for Easter Eve (ASB)

Surely he was the Son of God
MATTHEW 27.32–56

Any attempt at a comprehensive commentary on the passage which relates the crucifixion would be inadequate and my attempt more so than others. I shall therefore take three words from the account; the first by the evangelist, the second by Jesus on the cross, the third by the centurion and those with him.

1 *And sitting down, they kept watch over him there (v.36).* So far it has always been 'they' in our passage. The pronoun in fact refers back to the soldiers in v.27, but there is always an inclination to push all the blame back on 'they' and 'them'. It is easier to blame others and it avoids us getting too involved.

But there were many settling down to watch: the soldiers who after all were only doing their job, an easy and too frequent excuse we use for wrong-doing; the chief priests, the teachers of the law and the elders (v.41), enjoying their short hour of triumph, probably still feeling insecure (and we usually turn to mockery when we feel unsure of ourselves); the robbers crucified with him, even they 'heaped insults on him' (v.44), because they had to find some target for their anger (but see Luke 23.39–43); and then there were those who passed by (v.39) and it's too easy to hurl insults around when you are only passing by and don't give any commitment to living with what you have said, or thought, but are merely skating on the surface of life.

There were others: Simon who had carried Jesus' cross (v.32) and the many women who had ministered to the needs of Jesus and the disciples (vv.55f.), all faithful to the last. Friends—and foes. The cross of Jesus sorts people out; you cannot remain neutral and uncommitted. Friend or foe. As I watch, which will it be—for me?

2 *'My God, my God, why have you forsaken me?' (v.46).* These are the only recorded words of Jesus on the cross in Matthew's Gospel. The other six words are collated from the other Gospels. How interesting that Matthew recorded this, the most 'difficult' word. Of course it is the first verse of Psalm 22, which, if you examine it, you will find is an amazingly true description of the crucifixion and of what must have been Jesus' emotions. It is natural to look on it as the Psalm for Good Friday. But this outburst 'in a loud voice' was not that of a pious Jew reciting the Psalter. Or was it?

Jesus was giving expression to what he felt in the depths of his being. He was broken, dying, hardly able to speak. It would be intuitive to turn to a prayer of complaint, of lament, a prayer that we have too frequently neglected in Christian spirituality especially in modern times. (See Robert Faricy, SJ, *Praying for Inner Healing* (SCM), chapter 2, to which I am here indebted.) A Jew would know that several psalms are prayers of lament and this psalm (22) is one of them. They have a common structure:

a Calling out to the Lord.

b The complaint, expressive of inner feeling.

c An act of trust in the saving power of the Lord's love.

d A petition to be saved or to be healed.

e An act of praise and thanksgiving to the Lord for his compassion.

Perhaps this was the attempt Jesus made in his agony to remain in communion with, and within the will of, his heavenly Father. It is a prayer we could well return to, either using a psalm (e.g. 22, 42, 69, 102) or our own words after the above pattern. It helped Jesus in his hour of dereliction (it was nothing less) on the cross, 'the crucifixion within the crucifixion', and his prayer for healing was answered in the resurrection with life of a new order. This could be ours for the asking.

3 *'Surely he was the Son of God' (v.54)*. Mark and Luke mention the centurion only; Matthew relates the saying as a corporate testimony of the soldiers. They would not realize the significance of their words which were provoked by terror. A Christian can use the same words inspired by love and they become prophetic.

However, when all this is said, can we be so sure that something deeper did not stir within the hearts of those soldiers? Could anyone watch Jesus on the cross for six hours and remain unmoved? Could anyone be a spectator of that drama and come away unchanged? Could I? Or my friends? Even the most hard-bitten of us? Am I still unmoved, at this moment? How long can I maintain my pose of being able to rationalize every situation, of being clever and sophisticated, when I am confronted with divine reality, with him who is the Truth? Am I going to allow myself to feel his pull on my life, on me?

'But I, when I am lifted up from the earth, will draw all men to myself.' (John 12.32)

Recite slowly . Psalm 22

Prayer
Almighty Father,
look with mercy on this your family
for which our Lord Jesus Christ
 was content to be betrayed
 and given up into the hands of wicked men
 and to suffer death upon the cross;
who is alive and glorified
 with you and the Holy Spirit,
one God, now and for ever. Amen.
First Collect for Good Friday (ASB)

Sabbath rest
LUKE 23.50–6

The description of Joseph depicts a tough and saintly man: he was good, upright, did not go along with the crowd or majority decision, of a good Jewish settlement, a member of their Council, one who waited for the Kingdom of God (vv.50f.). He also had courage, for he went to Pilate to ask for Jesus' body; and he was generous, for presumably the tomb was his (v.53). And it all had to be done in a hurry, for it was the eve of the sabbath (v.54); the last rites had to be completed by sundown, but in this case the spices and perfumes were not ready (v.56). It is good that Joseph of Arimathea has a connection, however tenuous, with our country, in Glastonbury, and through the thorn tree with the Old Rectory at Crowhurst (where I am writing).

It is however the sabbath and the rest that must concern our hearts and minds today. Jesus rested in the grave on this day and *rest* in the Bible is an interesting idea. Originally denoting a cessation from labour (prior to further activity) it is then connected with peace, the opposite of turmoil of spirit and so becomes equivalent to death as the final cessation from strife. It is also connected with a place, e.g. the promised land.

Above all it is connected with God's creative activity which culminates in the saving work of Christ. Under the Old Covenant, God's people did not enter into his rest (Psalm 95), and so it belonged to the 'last days' which, because of Christ's redeeming work, have become 'today'. Jesus' message of the Kingdom in the future yet breaking into the present, has come true in his own person. He has entered into his rest and God's new creation can begin.

Coming from the root 'to desist', the *sabbath* may have been a lunar festival of joy and mirth, marked by abstention from normal business. It later became a weekly observance, marking the close of the seven-day week and it became a religious duty to keep it (the fourth commandment). The different sources of the Old Testament place various emphases on the sabbath's origin: one (D) connects it with deliverance from bondage (Deut. 5.12–15); another (P) with the rest of God after creation (Exod. 20.11); yet another (J) with the gift of manna (Exod. 16.22–30).

Jesus claimed a certain freedom from sabbath laws for himself and for his disciples (Mark 2.23–8), but a significant fact of his ministry was that he not only healed on the sabbath but almost went out of his way to do so (see the early chapters of Mark).

And when the inevitable opposition comes from the indignant voice of authority (e.g. Luke 13.14–17), Jesus infers that because it is a memorial of the peace (*shalom*) and rest which is God's, the sabbath is pre-eminently the day for fulfilling God's work of creation by bringing healing and wholeness to his people (John 7.23). It is from Jesus and not from the law that those who are heavy laden will receive the true sabbath rest. Furthermore, it seems likely from John 5.16–18 that the fourth evangelist saw in Jesus' healings on the sabbath a claim to be the Son of God because he was continuing God's work of creation. And again the author of Hebrews (in chapter 4) says that the life of Christian faith is a sabbath rest (4.9), secured by Christ, the high priest (4.14) in fulfilment of the Old Testament hope of a rest for the people of God.

So now Christ undergoes his own sabbath rest on the sabbath between his crucifixion and resurrection. It is traditional to think of him under the credal phrase, 'He descended into Hell', on this day. This is wholly appropriate on this day, the day when his Father ceased from the work of creation, but he continues that work (John 5.17) by bringing wholeness and healing to all souls, in this case those on the other side of the grave. He uses his sabbath rest as it were for the continuing purpose of the healing of his Father's creation. This is the sabbath rest, salvation/healing, that awaits the people of God, and is a necessary preparation for tomorrow's joyful resurrection.

Reflect on   1 Peter 3.17–end

Prayer

O Lord Jesus Christ, son of the living God, who at the evening hour rested in the sepulchre, and by this sanctified the grave to be a bed of hope to your people: Make us so to abound in sorrow for our sins, which were the cause of your Passion, that when our bodies lie in the dust, our souls may live with you; who lives and reigns with the Father and the Holy Spirit, one God, world without end.   Amen.

Collect for Compline

The day of resurrection

The time is now fulfilled: *today* is a day of celebration, the climax of all things—the day of resurrection, celebrated by Christians every Eastertide, every Sunday, always. 'God, you have brought joy to the whole world by the resurrection of your Son Jesus Christ from the dead.' That is why it is important to sing!

I propose that we reflect on Luke's account of the events of the first Easter Day, at leisure, slowly, in stillness and silence if possible (without therefore comment from me) and with joy in our hearts. After all, it *is* a special day, the day when the whole of creation was reborn overnight and a new order of things begun. Nothing and no one can be ever quite the same again. Can we? For the power that raised Jesus from the dead is available today for you and me, to empower us with life of a new order, the life that is in Christ Jesus our Lord. 'The old has gone, the new has come' (2 Cor. 5.17) as far as our life is concerned. How we shall want to praise him for that! Yes, we shall really want to 'set our hearts on things above, where Christ is seated at the right hand of God' (Col. 3.1).

Read (slowly)   Luke 24.1–53.

I want to end with a personal reminiscence. Before I was ordained, I was privileged to take part in a mission to Portsmouth. It was headed by Bishop Cuthbert Bardsley, and every parish had a missioner. Together with my fellow theological students from many colleges, I was placed in one of the parishes.

We learned a good deal, especially about house-to-house visiting, and it was good experience for us. I profited greatly from the nightly addresses of our missioner, now gone to his rest. In the first he gave, he asked us what sort of Christians we were. He told us he considered there were three types.

The first he called pre-crucifixion Christians, who thought a great deal about Jesus as a good person and teacher. The classic expression of this view can be found in today's reading (vv.19–21). But there some people stay, with just a happy memory and no life to carry them on into the future.

The second he called crucifixion Christians, those who really did come to the foot of the cross, who knew the saving benefits of the crucified Lord, as a result of which they received great comfort. However they tended to remain there instead of receiving new life to rise up and go on life's journey.

The third he called post-crucifixion Christians who went forward from the cross, through the grave and gate of death, holding Christ's hand and passing to the joy and new life of the resurrection. They are given a new radiance by the risen Lord, a new purpose to their life, a new zest for living which can be an inspiration and help to others and assist in the forward movement of God's Kingdom. Inevitably they will still face the stresses and suffering life brings, but with new attitudes, new purpose and an unquenchable joy.

He then faced us with the question: in which group do you see yourself? Well? Let us pray for grace to be true children of the resurrection.

Read   1 Peter 1.3–9

Concluding prayer
    Risen Lord, we meet with joy on this day of resurrection.
        As we celebrate your triumph
            we pray your joy may abide in our hearts,
            and that our lives may proclaim your praise;
    Be our unseen companion along the daily journey of our life, and at the ending of the day come and abide with us in our dwellings; for your love's sake.   Amen.
Adapted from two prayers by Frank Colquhoun

GROUP QUESTIONS

Christ's own adventure

1 'The destructive force of anger must always go hand in hand with the healing power of love.' How do we use our anger? Does it go hand in hand with love and issue in reconciliation? (Sunday 6)

2 'Who do you say I am?' What answer would we give? (Monday). How would our answer affect our understanding of the teaching Jesus gave on discipleship? (Matt. 16.24–7)

3 How far do our 'disclosure moments' (cf. the disciples' experience at the Transfiguration—Tuesday) assist and equip us for the adventure of the 'plain'?

4 How greatly do we perceive and value the 'timeless potency' of the Eucharist? In our celebration of this sacrament, do we enjoy the experience of being caught up into the dimension of eternity? 'Therefore with angels and archangels and with all the company of heaven . . .' (Wednesday)

5 Are we able to face the prospect of dying and of death trustfully, hopefully, courageously? (Thursday)

6 Read 1 Cor. 1.22–5. How can we most effectively preach Christ crucified to today's world?

7 The idea of re-creation on the sabbath is now applicable to the Christian day of resurrection, Sunday. How healing and re-creating is our Sunday? If it is not, what have we lost from the observance of 'the day of rest'?

8 In which of the three categories do you see yourself? If the third, how conscious are you of the power of Christ's resurrection as well as of the fellowship of his sufferings? See Phil. 3.10. (Sunday 7)

EPILOGUE

And what now? What new adventure awaits us? Surely the exciting business of living—living life to the full, the very purpose for which Christ came (John 10.10).

That means we have to keep very close to him; and that means being constant in prayer (Rom. 12.12). These heroes of faith in the Christian adventure were all great men and women of prayer, which was no mere 'extra' they managed to find time for in their busy lives. *It was* their lives. They lived prayer, because every breath they breathed was an inhalation of the Spirit of God, every step they took was in his footsteps, every heartbeat was in tune with the divine rhythm, every thought and action was enfolded in his love and offered in accordance with his will. Herein lay for them the great adventure.

'Prayer catapults us onto the frontier of the spiritual life,' writes Richard Foster in his great little book on the spiritual life (*Celebration of Discipline*, p.30), 'it is original research in unexplored territory . . . prayer itself brings us into the deepest and highest work of the human spirit. Real prayer is life creating and life changing . . . To pray is to change. Prayer is the central avenue God uses to transform us.'

We shall remember how it was Luke's perception that the Transfiguration of our Lord took place in the context of prayer. Prayer and Transfiguration, transformation, go together. To pray is indeed to change and if we don't want to change, let's avoid prayer at all costs!

But change lies at the heart of the Christian adventurer whose purpose is to be transformed into the likeness of Jesus. *Let our spiritual exercises together give us the discipline of being constantly open and receptive to the beam of God's love upon us and of allowing that love to change us at the centre.* Let God's love and joy and peace, and health and wholeness and holiness, sink down into our deep mind, permeating our whole being and crowding out all that is bad and rotten and sinful. What a transformation will take place!

Then, with our personality burnished like a mirror (Aelred of Rievaulx likened Christians to 'mirrors of charity'), let us reflect something of this strong love of God on to others, on to all whom we meet. How a smile can light up a room and change an atmosphere. So can prayer. Let us undertake the adventure of beaming the love of God silently with our eyes on all whom we see and come in contact with today, tomorrow . . . on all we meet travelling to work, at work, at leisure, in our home, in our church (especially the preacher as he preaches the word to us—how it will improve his/her sermons!) and everywhere we find ourselves. There are too many words in the world: the joy of serving *the* Word can often best be conveyed by non-verbal communication.

So let us reflect on to others the strong rays of love God beams on to us. What ambassadors we shall be! How we shall live life to the full—for the greater glory of God. How also we shall be humbled, as are all God's servants—and tested.

Herein therefore lies the Christian adventure for us: so to be open to the transforming love of God in prayer that we are gradually changed into his likeness 'from glory to glory advancing'. Then shall we be his mirrors of love. May our work together in these six weeks help forward this advance and set us firmly once more on the road of the Christian adventure.

'Spirit of the living God, fall afresh on me.'   Amen.

ACKNOWLEDGEMENTS

Biblical quotations in this book are from the New International Version of the Bible, copyright © 1978 by New York International Bible Society, first published in Great Britain in 1979, and are used by permission.

The Collects from The Alternative Service Book 1980 (marked ASB) and the Collect 'O Lord Jesus Christ, Son of the Living God . . .' (as adapted) from Compline in the 1928 Prayer Book are © The Central Board of Finance of the Church of England, and are reproduced by permission.

Extracts from the Book of Common Prayer of 1662 (marked BCP), which is Crown Copyright, are used by permission.

Extracts from *Contemporary Parish Prayers* and *Parish Prayers* by Frank Colquhoun are reprinted by permission of Hodder and Stoughton Limited.

The extract from *The Pain that Heals* by Martin Israel is reprinted by permission of Hodder and Stoughton Limited.

Extracts from *Be Still and Know* by Michael Ramsey are reprinted by permission of William Collins Limited.